FRENCH
JoKe BooK

500 Puns Guaranteed to
Give You Déjà-Eww!

Sue Fenton

New York   Chicago   San Francisco   Lisbon   London   Madrid   Mexico City
Milan   New Delhi   San Juan   Seoul   Singapore   Sydney   Toronto

The **McGraw·Hill** Companies

Library of Congress Cataloging-in-Publication Data

Fenton, Sue.
    The world's wackiest French joke book : 500 puns guaranteed to give you
deja-eww! / Sue Fenton.
        p.   cm.
    ISBN 0-07-147900-7
    1. Puns and printing.   2. French language—Humor.

  PN6231.P8 F45   2006
  448.102/07—dc22   2006048102

Dedicated to my loving family,
my wonderful friends,
and the playful spirit in all of us.

1 2 3 4 5 6 7 8 9 10 11 12 13 14 15 16 17 18   FGR/FGR   0 9 8 7 6

ISBN-13: 978-0-07-147900-4
ISBN-10:   0-07-147900-7

Interior design by Think Design Group, LLC
Interior artwork by Luc Nisset

McGraw-Hill books are available at special quantity discounts to use as premiums
and sales promotions, or for use in corporate training programs. For more
information, please write to the Director of Special Sales, Professional Publishing,
McGraw-Hill, Two Penn Plaza, New York, NY 10121-2298. Or contact your local
bookstore.

This book is printed on acid-free paper.

BONJOUR!

Welcome to this wacky (or "waqué") collection of five hundred jokes and puns with a French twist! It's a celebration of the beautiful French language, and you're invited to join the "franco-fun."

The jokes are asked in English and the answers playfully fracture French and warp pronunciations. There is also a big dose of "franglais"—words that mix French and English. The jokes are sprinkled with pop culture confetti from both sides of the Atlantic. From Harry Potter, to Oreos, Louis XIV, Bazooka, Auguste Renoir, iPods, Benjamin Franklin, French pastries, Fruit of the Loom, or French cheese—anything goes!

Some of the jokes are based on America's general awareness of French and France. Others require some knowledge of French, but if you get stumped there are vocabulary notes to help you. While your mind is being challenged and teased, you can dust off your French or learn some more French, and find out some trivia about France at the same time.

Get yourself some French fries, chocolate éclairs, or crêpes Suzette. Then relax and let yourself get a little crazy. Be prepared for some entertaining "haute quizzing," and expect the unexpected. May you chuckle with a French accent and have many "oh là là laughs."

GROAN VOYAGE!

DID YOU KNOW THAT FRENCH . . .

- was the official language of England for three hundred years? William the Conqueror of France defeated Harold of England in the Battle of Hastings in 1066 and won the throne that had been promised to him. That's when they started speaking French in England.

- is responsible for up to 50 percent of the English vocabulary, according to linguists, and that it brought Latin influences to English, too?

- is an official language of the United Nations, UNESCO, the International Olympic Committee, the International Red Cross, NATO, and the International Postal Union?

- is spoken by almost 200 million people on six continents?

- is spoken in 43 countries, by 67 million people as a first language and 128 million people as a second language?

- has thousands of cognates—French words that look just like English words?

SAY WHAT?

Here are some pronunciation tips to help you with new French words:

Vowels

a, â	UH	b<u>u</u>bble
e	EH	k<u>e</u>tchup
e (end of word)	Silent!	
é, ez, et, ed, er, ai	AY	sk<u>a</u>te
i, y	EE	p<u>i</u>zza
o (with a consonant)	Ŏ	<u>o</u>ctopus
o (before "s" or the last sound)	OH	n<u>o</u>se
u	EE + OOH (blended)	<u>few</u>
au, aux, eau, eaux	OH	<u>oa</u>ts
eu, eux	EUH	p<u>er</u>fect
ou, oux	OOH	p<u>oo</u>dle
oi	WUH	<u>wa</u>ffle

Consonants

Consonants at the end of words are *not* pronounced except for C, R, F, and L. French consonants are pronounced like English ones with these exceptions:

c + a, o, u	K	<u>c</u>omedy
c + e, i	SS	<u>c</u>ircus
ç	SS	<u>s</u>paghetti
ch	SH	<u>sh</u>ampoo
g + a,o,u	G	<u>g</u>litter
g + e, i	ZH	colla<u>ge</u>

gn	NYA	ca**ny**on
h	Silent!	
j	ZH	trea**s**ure
qu	K	**k**ite
r	KH (at the back of the throat)	Ba**ch**
s (between vowels)	Z	ro**s**e
s	SS	**s**ailboat
th	T	**t**rumpet
x	KSS	ta**x**i
	SS ("six" and "dix")	**x**ylophone

Nasals

an, am en, em	AH(N)	**un**real
in, im, ein, ain, aim	EH(N)	v**an**
on, om	OH(N)	**ow**n
un, um	URH(N)	**ear**n

Here is how you chuckle in French:

HÉ! HÉ! HÉ!

(HA! HA! HA!)

AGNEAU MARK, GET SET, GO!

THE MENU OF JOKES
★
Le menu des blagues

GROAN APPÉTIT!

ANIMALS

Les animaux

What does a French official say to start the 200-meter dash for **lamb**s?

★ **"Agneau** mark, get set, go!" *(On your mark; un agneau = lamb)*

    FUN FACT: "Doux comme un agneau" means "sweet as a lamb."

Why do French **turkey**s use Head and Shoulders?

★ *Because they have **dinde**-druff. (dandruff; une dinde = turkey hen)*

    FUN FACT: A male turkey in French is "un dindon." A baby turkey is "un dindonneau." "Gobble Gobble" is "Glouglou Glouglou."

What is the most common name for a French **camel**?

★ *Joe **Chameau** (Joe Schmoe; un chameau = camel)*

What saying do you get when you cross Obi-wan Kenobi with a French **bear**?

★ *"May the **ours** be with you."* *(force; un ours = bear)*

   FUN FACT: A teddy bear in French is a "nounours." Its nickname is "doudou."

What was the final battle between a French **beaver** and land developers who wanted to bulldoze its dam?

★ **Castor**'s Last Stand *(Custer's; un castor = beaver)*

   FUN FACT: A "queue de castor" or "beaver's tail" is a long fried pastry from Quebec. It has cinnamon and sugar or other toppings on it.

What is the favorite perfume of a French **cat**?

★ **Chat**-nel #5 *(Chanel #5; un chat = cat)*

   FUN FACT: Artists Claude Monet and Auguste Renoir; composers Maurice Ravel, Frédéric Chopin, and Camille Saint-Saëns; writers Colette and Jules Verne; and statesman Cardinal Richelieu . . . all loved cats.

What countries do the French call the upper and lower halves of King Kong's body?

★ *North and South **Gorille*** *(North and South Korea; un gorille = gorilla)*

What does a French **horse** trainer take with her to the beach?

★ *a pail and a **cheval*** *(shovel; un cheval = horse)*

FUN FACT: Chantilly is the horse capital of France. The prince of Condé, who lived at the Château of Chantilly, expected to be reincarnated as a horse and built magnificent stables for himself there. "Hiiiii! Hiiiii!" ("Neigh! "Neigh!") The prince says, "Bonjour."

What make of car does a French **goat** drive?

★ *a **Chèvre**-olet* *(Chevrolet; une chèvre = female goat)*

FUN FACT: "La Chèvre de Monsieur Seguin" by Alphonse Daudet is a story about a little goat that runs away from its yard. It frolics in the mountains . . . until it meets a hungry wolf. Moral: It's better to be safe than to be an entrée.

A French goat cruises in his Chèvre-olet.

What French cartoon **pig** would you not want to put in a room full of balloons?

★ **Porc**-épic *(Porky Pig; un porc-épic = porcupine)*

On what holiday do French **whale**s send each other candy and flowers?

★ on **Baleine**-tine's day *(Valentine's; une baleine = whale)*

What do the French call trying to figure out what's on a **goat**'s mind?

★ reading a **bouc** *(book; un bouc = male goat)*

FUN FACT: "Un bouc" is also a goatee or small beard on a man's chin. Djali is the name of Esmeralda's goat in *The Hunchback of Notre Dame.* And remember, you can't judge a "bouc" by its cover.

What do French cats say when they greet each other?

★ *"Chalut!"* *(salut = hi; un chat = cat)*

FUN FACT: Composer Frédéric Chopin based "The Cat's Waltz" on a little melody his cat created when it strutted across the keys of his piano.

When does a French **steer** get to blow out candles on a cake?

★ on his **bœuf**day *(birthday; un bœuf = steer)*

What French record company produces albums of **sheep** singing R&B and soul?

★ **Mouton** *(Motown; un mouton = sheep)*

> **FUN FACT:** "Le mouton à cinq pattes" (the five-footed sheep) refers to something that's impossible to find or does not exist. It also means last season's designer fashion discounts. There's a chain of boutiques in Paris named Mouton à Cinq Pattes where affordable designer bargains can be found.

What island city is known for its French hula-dancing wolves?

★ Hono**loup**loup *(Honolulu; un loup = wolf)*

> **FUN FACT:** In France you can be hungry as a wolf. "J'ai une faim de loup" means "I'm starving." A werewolf in French is a "loup-garou."

Vacationing in HonoLoupLoup

Why can't you ever depend on a French **donkey**?

★ *It's never **âne** time and it's **âne**-reliable* (on time; unreliable; un âne = donkey)

> **FUN FACT:** "Têtu comme un âne" means "stubborn as a mule."

How did the French **cow** that was dressed up for the senior prom look?

★ *ra-**vache**-ing* (ravishing; une vache = cow)

> **FUN FACT:** Normandy is known for its cows and dairy products.

"I look ra-vache-ing, n'est-ce pas?"

For what is a French **dog** best known?

★ *its in-**chien**-uity* (ingenuity; un chien = dog)

> **FUN FACT:** There are 7.3 million pet dogs in France. A doggy is a "toutou." The French king Henri IV said, "Love me, love my dog."

What did the announcer at the French dog competition say when a performing **puppy** stopped walking?

⋆ *"The **chiot** must go on."* *(show; un chiot = puppy)*

> **FUN FACT:** Dingo is the French name for Disney's cartoon dog, Goofy.

What small metal or plastic figurines of brave **pig**s do French boys play with and collect?

⋆ *ac-**cochon** heroes* *(action heroes; un cochon = pig)*

How does the French poodle's version of *Moby Dick* begin?

⋆ *"Call me Can-Ishmael."* *(un caniche = poodle)*

> **FUN FACT:** French poodles have been used for duck hunting, finding truffles, circus entertainment, court pets, and as guide dogs. The poodle is "très intelligent."

What French sea creature is red and says, "D'eau"?

⋆ **Homard** *Simpson* *(un homard = lobster; "Doh"; d'eau = of water)*

What does a polite French **mouse** say when it accidentally steps on your foot?

⋆ *"I'm so **souris**."* *(sorry; une souris = mouse)*

> **FUN FACT:** Instead of a tooth fairy, a mouse visits French children to collect their teeth. Children ask, "Est-ce que la petite souris est passée?" (Did the little mouse come?)

What do you call the French **dog**s that grew up with computers and the World Wide Web?

★ *the Net **Chien**-eration* (Net Generation; un chien = dog)

FUN FACT: A "cynophile" is a French person who loves dogs.

What NFL team is made up of French **guinea pigs**?

★ *the Dallas **Cobayes*** (Cowboys; un cobaye = guinea pig)

What does a **cat** order from in a French restaurant?

★ *the **minou*** (menu; un minou = cat, kitty)

FUN FACT: "Minou" is a French child's word for "kitty." It's also used when you don't know a cat's name. "Viens, minou" means "Here, kitty kitty." Gros Minet is Sylvester the Cat in France. Tweety is Titi.

What do French hippos take when they have heartburn?

★ *a Hippopo-TUM* (TUMS; un hippopotame = hippopotamus)

Why does a French **fish** have so many friends?

★ *Because it has a great **poisson**-ality.* (personality; un poisson = fish)

What did the French **ant** say when her friend handed her a gift?

★ *"**Fourmi**?"* (For me; une fourmi = ant)

What French **cat** was an emperor of the Franks?

★ ***Chat**-lemagne (Charlemagne; un chat = cat)*

> **FUN FACT:** Speaking of emperors, Napoléon Bonaparte did not like cats.

What do you call it when French zookeepers keep **monkey**s from speaking their minds?

★ ***singe**-sorship (censorship; un singe = monkey)*

What do the French call a **dog** that runs for public office?

★ *a politi-**chien** (politician; un chien = dog)*

"Biscuits for everyone," promised the French politi-chien.

ART

L'art

What do the employees at a French gift wrap department study?

★ *the beaux-arts (bows; beaux arts = fine arts)*

> **FUN FACT:** The French École des Beaux-Arts (School of Fine Arts) was founded in Paris by Cardinal Mazarin in 1648. Today it trains students from all over the world.

What did the server at the eighteenth-century artist café say when customers asked for a Coke?

★ *"Sorry, but we only serve Roco Cola here." (Rococo = eighteenth-century style)*

> **FUN FACT:** Rococo was a playful, frilly, decorative eighteenth-century style. Aristocrats were shown frolicking in forests in fancy ruffles, shiny silks, and fluffy dresses. Clocks, furniture, and china were made in the elegant Rococo style in bright colors with gold accents.

What does a French artist spray on a **drawing** to get rid of germs?

★ a **dessin**-fectant *(disinfectant; un dessin = drawing)*

What do you call an Australian mammal that gets loose in a French artist's studio and has paint all over its bill?

★ a **palette**-ypus *(platypus; une palette = an artist's tool for holding dabs of paints)*

What do French Munchkin artists sing when they're looking for **green** paint?

★ *"Some-**vert** O-**vert** the Rainbow"* *(Somewhere Over; vert = green)*

FUN FACT: Scholars speculate that some Impressionist artists like Monet, Cézanne, and van Gogh developed physical conditions because they were poisoned by their bright green paint. It contained "Paris Green," a poisonous pigment with arsenic that was used to kill rats in the Paris sewers and was also put into insecticides.

What did the art critic say when he saw Monet's hazy **blue** painting of the Rouen Cathedral?

★ *"It's all a **bleu** to me."* *(blur; bleu = blue)*

FUN FACT: Monet did a series of thirty paintings of the Rouen cathedral and painted a series of haystacks and water lilies. He was interested in the effects of light at different times of the day.

What did the French man shout when he saw lit firecrackers attached to a **painting**?

★ *"Run! She's about **tableau**!"* *(to blow; un tableau = painting)*

FUN FACT: The painting titled *The Coronation of Napoleon* by Jacques-Louis David in the Louvre is enormous. It's twenty feet by thirty-two feet in size.

A museum visitor is alarmed by a painting.

What French hero was **yellow** and quacked?

★ ***Jaune*** *Duck (Jeanne D'Arc = Joan of Arc, French heroine from Domrémy)*

FUN FACT: Joan of Arc (1412–1431) heard voices at thirteen, convinced Charles VII to give her an army, and rallied the French to victory over the English. She was struck in the shoulder by an arrow during the fighting but pulled it out and continued on. French traitors gave her to the English, who burned her alive while she wore a cap labeled "heretic."

What American president was known for wearing French **blush** on his cheeks?

★ *Teddy **Rouge**-evelt (Roosevelt; rouge = red, blush)*

FUN FACT: The gorgeous red in the décor of Versailles Palace and in the red robes of Louis XIV came from bugs.

What should a French artist and stockholder do when her palette has only two shades of **green**?

★ *di-**vert**-sify (diversify; vert = green)*

FUN FACT: During the Middle Ages green was worn by the insane. If you wore green during the French Revolution, you could be beaten or arrested. In France a flashing green cross mounted on a building is a sign for a pharmacy.

What do French **watercolor** artists have when they lose their tempers?

★ ***aquarelle** (a quarrel; une aquarelle = watercolor)*

FUN FACT: The paint tube, invented in 1841, allowed French Impressionists to paint outside. Auguste Renoir said, "Without tubes of paint, there would have been no Impressionism."

On what does a French spider artist both paint and hang out?

★ *a **toile** (une toile = canvas, spiderweb)*

What treats do French people give their art connoisseur dogs?

★ **Louvre** *Snaps* *(liver snaps; Louvre = Paris art museum that opened in 1793)*

FUN FACT: The Louvre has 200,000 works (30,000 exhibited) from antiquity to 1848. When Hitler approached Paris, thousands of works were hidden all over France, even in haylofts. When France was liberated, every work of art was returned.

What did Leonardo da Vinci use to make copies of sketches of his famous lady?

★ *a **Mona** laser printer (Mona Lisa = Leonardo da Vinci painting at the Louvre)*

FUN FACT: *Mona Lisa*, or *La Joconde* to the French, is Monna Lisa del Giocondo from Florence, Italy. She's only 31" x 21". Mona likes a temperature of 68°F with 55 percent humidity. Each year 300,000 *Mona Lisa* cards and souvenirs are sold at the Louvre.

What did the French artist Jean-François Millet do with his dirty shirts every week?

★ *He took them to The **Gleaners**. (cleaners; The Gleaners = painting by Millet)*

FUN FACT: Jean-François Millet (1814–1875) respected hard work and painted peasant farm laborers as if they were noble heroes. At that time, only wealthy people were considered worthy subjects for paintings. He spent many years in debt, hungry and depressed.

What did Leonardo da Vinci's famous lady put on to unwind after the museum closed?

★ *a ki-Mona (kimono;* Mona Lisa*)*

> **FUN FACT:** The *Mona Lisa* was stolen in 1911 and was missing for twenty-seven months until the thief tried to sell her in Italy and was caught. Most of those two years she spent right in Paris in apartments not far from the Louvre. Pablo Picasso was once a suspect in the theft.

What group of French landscape artists painted dolls?

★ *the Barbie-zon School (Barbizon = a school for landscape painters)*

> **FUN FACT:** The Barbizon School (1830–1870) attracted painters like Millet and Corot who glorified nature and the countryside. The school was set in the woods of Fontainebleau.

After Barbie broke up with her seventeenth-century French boyfriend, how did he paint?

★ *with a **Baroque**-Ken heart (Baroque = seventeenth-century art style)*

> **FUN FACT:** Baroque art, music, and sculpture were busy and grabbed your attention. Statues were frozen in the middle of action. Baroque gardens were huge, had many fountains, and were used for elegant parties.

What do the French call painting with a baguette?

★ *la painture (le pain = bread; la peinture = painting (action); une baguette = loaf of crusty French bread)*

Why did Mr. Lautrec's easel keep falling down?

★ *Because the screws were too loose.* (Toulouse; Henri de Toulouse-Lautrec)

FUN FACT: Toulouse-Lautrec (1864–1901) fractured both thigh bones in accidents at ages twelve and fourteen, causing his legs to stop growing. As a man, he had a normal torso but short legs and was only 4' 6". He walked with a cane and wore a black hat and monocle.

What was the front-page headline of the Copenhagen newspaper when the French sculpture, *The Thinker*, arrived?

★ *"Something's **Rodin** in Denmark."* (rotten; Rodin = sculptor of Le Penseur)

FUN FACT: Auguste Rodin (1840–1917) originally named this sculpture *The Poet.* It sits amid rosebushes in front of the Musée Rodin in Paris.

What did the thief say to his partners when they broke into the French Impressionist art museum?

★ *"Quick! Take the **Monet** and run."* (money; Monet = Impressionist artist)

FUN FACT: Claude Monet (1840–1926) received a negative critique of his painting *Impression: Sunrise*, which led to the artistic term "Impressionism." Monet built a floating studio at Giverny so he could see the reflections on his pond up close when he painted. Monet had ten children, loved to cook, and once won the French lottery.

When the French artist of the cabarets bought his Chevy pickup, what did he promise never to do?

★ *Toulouse Le Truck* (to lose; Toulouse-Lautrec)

FUN FACT: Toulouse-Lautrec (1864–1901) was a Postimpressionist artist. He lived on Montmartre and painted social outcasts and cabaret singers and dancers. His flat coloring-book style with simple outlines of people made him the father of the poster.

What is a pass to a series of Postimpressionist art exhibits in Aix-en-Provence called?

★ a **Cézanne** ticket (season; Paul Cézanne = Postimpressionist artist)

FUN FACT: Paul Cézanne (1839–1906) painted objects and people with solid geometric shapes, which led to Cubism. He came from Aix-en-Provence and is said to have painted pictures of the nearby mountain, Mont Sainte-Victoire, 450 times.

Who lived under Paris and painted with hundreds of tiny dots?

★ *Georges Sewer-rat* (Seurat; un rat = rat)

FUN FACT: Georges Seurat (1859–1891) studied color through the science of optics and used tiny dots. His style is called Pointillism. He did five hundred sketches, but only seven paintings because it took such a long time to paint all those dots.

What did the modern French artist from Nice tell his dentist after the drilling was done?

★ *"**Matisse** hurt!"* *(my teeth; Matisse = father of modern art)*

> **FUN FACT:** Henri Matisse (1869–1954) was a Fauve (wild beast) artist who painted forms in bright colors without outlines. Matisse inspired modern wallpaper designs. His painting *The Boat* was hung upside down by mistake in a New York museum for a month and a half.

What French artist owned a store that sold foul-weather gear?

★ *Auguste Rainwear (Renoir = Impressionist artist)*

> **FUN FACT:** Auguste Renoir (1841–1919) painted people—especially women and children—in the Impressionist style. Renoir spent his last twenty years in a wheelchair. Because of his arthritis, he had to have brushes strapped to his hands so he could paint.

What lullaby did the French Cubist painter's mother sing to him when he was in his cradle?

★ *"**Braque**-a-bye Baby . . ."* *(Rock; Georges Braque – pioneer of Cubism)*

> **FUN FACT:** Georges Braque (1882–1963) divided his subjects into geometric shapes and mixed them up. The spectator had to sort it all out. Braque and Picasso were the first artists to do collages. His favorite vegetable was, of course, "Braque-oli."

The World's Wackiest French Joke Book

What French Impressionist's paintings go well with cold cuts?

★ **Manet's** *(mayonnaise; Édouard Manet = artist who inspired Impressionism)*

> **FUN FACT:** Édouard Manet (1832–1883) painted *Music in the Tuileries*. The people in the park are his friends, artists, musicians, authors, and himself. He shows that in the distance, objects become blurred by the atmosphere, light, dust, or smoke.

Where did the French artist who painted ballet dancers buy his jeans?

★ *at De-Gap (Degas; The Gap)*

> **FUN FACT:** Edgar Degas (1834–1917) painted people at their jobs like laundry ladies, hat makers, and ballet dancers. Legend has it Degas removed some remains in a family vault in the Montmartre cemetery to make room for himself.

What did van Gogh tell his artist friend to do when they were playing "Go Fish" in the yellow house in Arles and his friend got a pair?

★ *"Paul, go a-guin." (go again; Paul Gauguin = Postimpressionist artist)*

> **FUN FACT:** Paul Gauguin (1848–1903) traveled the world with the French navy, lived in Tahiti, and painted exotic women. He joined Vincent van Gogh in southern France, but they always argued. He left, and an upset Vincent cut off part of his own ear.

What did people exclaim when a Plymouth Voyager with the painting *Starry Night* on the side of it went speeding by?

★ *"Wow! Look at that van go!"* (Vincent van Gogh = Postimpressionist artist)

FUN FACT: Vincent van Gogh (1853–1890) did 750 paintings and 1,600 drawings in ten years. He painted fields, sunflowers, portraits, and stars and painted forty self-portraits. Among his most famous paintings are *The Potato Eaters* and *Starry Night.* Vincent spoke four languages. He was born a year to the day after another baby brother, also named Vincent, who died at birth.

The painting *Starry Night* sped past the tourists.

BIRDS

★

Les oiseaux

Why didn't the French boy get the joke about the **bird**?

★ It **oiseau**-ver his head. *(was over; un oiseau = bird)*

> **FUN FACT:** Toccata is the white French cousin of Big Bird on "1, Rue Sésame." The cast also includes Mordicus, a grouch who lives in a "poubelle" (trash can); Trépido, a snail; and Ernest and Bart.

What video game system does a French **chicken** have?

★ a **Poulet** Station *(Play Station; un poulet = chicken)*

What do you call a French **swan** that is over sixty-five?

★ a **cygne** citizen *(senior; un cygne = swan)* It sometimes has cygne moments.

> **FUN FACT:** Throughout the centuries, swans have graced the moats and ponds of many French châteaux.

What would you call seeing a French **eagle** in a pink tutu riding on a skateboard?

★ *highly irr-**aigle*** *(irregular; un aigle = eagle)*

Who treats a crazy French **quail** when it needs therapy?

★ *a psy-**caille**-atrist* *(psychiatrist; une caille = quail)*

What does a French **owl** wear when it goes jogging on cool days?

★ *a **chouette** shirt* *(sweat; une chouette = owl)*

FUN FACT: The word for "awesome" in French is also "chouette." The jogging owl could, therefore, wear a "chouette chouette" shirt.

In what region of France do many geese live?

★ *in the L'Oie Valley* *(Loire Valley; une oie = goose)*

FUN FACT: The French expression "bête comme une oie" means "silly as a goose."

What do French bird-watchers say when they spot a **woodpecker** from behind a tree?

★ *"**Pic**-a-boo."* *(Peek; un pic = woodpecker)*

FUN FACT: Hide-and-seek in French is "Cache-cache."

What does the umpire shout to start a game in which French **chicken**s run around four bases?

★ *"**Poulet** ball!"* ("Play ball!"; un poulet = chicken)

> **FUN FACT:** Le Poulet Frit du Kentucky (PFK) has restaurants in France. They serve "les Tenders" and "le Bucket." The chicken is "original" or "épicé" (spicy).

Why didn't the French **crow**'s friends laugh at his jokes?

★ *Because they were too **corneille**.* (corny; une corneille = crow)

What does a pink French bird with long legs dance when it's on vacation in Spain?

★ *the **flamant**-co* (flamenco; un flamant = flamingo)

> **FUN FACT:** The Camargue region of France near the Mediterranean coast is a region of marshlands with wild flamingos, horses, and bulls.

What do the French shout when a **sparrow** falls off a boat?

★ *"**Moineau**-ver board!"* ("Man overboard!"; un moineau = sparrow)

> **FUN FACT:** The legendary world-renowned French singer, Édith Piaf, was called "Le Petit Moineau." The French use "un piaf" as a synonym for "sparrow."

Where does a French **hen** do the breaststroke?

★ *in a swimming **poule*** (pool; une poule = hen)

FUN FACT: "Quand les poules auront les dents" (when hens have teeth) means "when pigs fly." Goose bumps are "la chair de poule" (hen flesh).

How do Spanish people address an unmarried French lady **swan**?

★ *"**Cygne**-rita."* ("Señorita"; un cygne = swan)

What French bird was the first James Bond?

★ *Sean **Canari*** (Sean Connery; un canari = canary)

Was it love at first sight for the female French **crane**?

★ *No, her boyfriend slowly **grue** on her.* (grew; une grue = crane)

What French bird lives on Alsace rooftops and starred in *Alien*?

★ ***Cigogne** Weaver* (Sigourney; une cigogne = stork)

FUN FACT: Storks build nests on the rooftops of homes in the region of Alsace.

Why did the teacher send the French **ostrich** to the principal's office?

★ *Because of its **autruche**-ious behavior.* (atrocious; une autruche = ostrich)

What line of a holiday song do you get when a French partridge swallows another **partridge**?

★ *"And a partridge in a **perdrix**."* *(pear tree; un perdrix = partridge)*

What did the French **raven**'s nutritionist tell him to do?

★ *to go on a low-**corbeau**-hydrate diet* *(low-carbohydrate; un corbeau = raven)*

Why does a French **skylark** wipe itself with a towel when it gets out of a pool?

★ *Because it's **alouette**.* *(all wet; une alouette = skylark)*

FUN FACT: The French children's song "Alouette" is about plucking the feathers off a bird's body. "Aie!" (Ouch!) Alouette is also a French radio station.

What do French fans of Edgar Allan Poe's "The **Raven**" put on a wrapped gift?

★ *a **corbeau*** *(bow; un corbeau = raven)*

Where is a teenage French **parrot** educated?

★ *at a **perroquet**-al school* *(parochial; un perroquet = parrot)*

FUN FACT: During World War I, parrots were used for audio surveillance on the Eiffel Tower. They could hear enemy planes in the distance before any humans could. The artist Cézanne taught his parrot to say, "Paul Cézanne est un grand peintre." (Paul Cézanne is a great painter.)

BODY

★

Le corps

How does the anatomy department at the French university start its invitations for an open house?

★ *"You are **corps**-dially invited . . . "* *(cordially; le corps = body)*

What character from *Gone with the Wind* is all bones?

★ **Squelette** *O'Hara (Scarlett; un squelette = skeleton)*

FUN FACT: Most French words that end in "-ette" are feminine in gender and would have "la" in front of them. "Le squelette" is an exception.

Which former "Today" show host has a big **heart**?

★ *Katie **Cœur**-ic (Couric; un cœur = heart)*

What kind of car do French podiatrists drive?

★ *a **Cheville** (Chevy; une cheville = ankle)*

What does a French neurosurgeon say when her
assistants are bickering?

★ *"A **nerf** is a **nerf**."* (enough; un nerf = nerve)

What do French optometrists say at their wedding
ceremonies?

★ *"**Œil** do."* ("I do"; un œil = eye)

FUN FACT: The expression "Mon œil!" means "No way!"

Where in Europe do French dermatologists go to study?

★ *They go to **Peau**-land.* (Poland; la peau = skin)

FUN FACT: In English people risk their necks. In French they
risk their skin. The expression is "risquer sa peau."

What do French people use to scour their belly buttons?

★ *nom-Brillo pads* (un nombril = belly button)

FUN FACT: The bikini, which appeared in the late 1940s, was
sometimes called the "nombril" because it exposed the belly
button. "Nombril" referred to the lower portion of the bikini and
is still used today as a name for a style of underwear.

What do French manufacturers of rubber **ear**s shout to
celebrate record sales?

★ *"Hip hip **oreille**."* (hurray; une oreille = ear)

FUN FACT: The French expression "avoir quelque chose entre
les oreilles" means "to have something between your ears," in
other words, to be smart.

What do the French call a tight muscle in your **back**?

★ a **dos** knot *(donut; le dos = back)*

   FUN FACT: The phrase for the square-dancing step called a "do-si-do" comes from the French "dos à dos" meaning a back-to-back turn.

Why do the French think people should **comb** their hair instead of going to war?

★ *They believe the **peigne** is mightier than the sword.* *(pen; un peigne = comb)*

What do the French call getting **bangs** trimmed with a haircut?

★ **frange** benefits *(fringe; une frange = bangs)*

Where do French shoppers buy their turtle**neck** sweaters?

★ at J. **Cou** *(J. Crew; le cou = neck)*

   FUN FACT: A "cou de girafe" is a long neck and a "cou de taureau" (bull) is a thick, strong neck.

What do the French call a person who talks too much?

★ **langue**-winded *(long-winded; une langue = tongue)*

   FUN FACT: A popular French cookie is the "langue de chat" (cat's tongue). It's a butter cookie shaped like a cat's tongue that is sometimes dipped in chocolate.

What did the French **hair** stylist do when she saw a ghost in her hair salon?

★ *She began to* **cheveux**. *(shiver; les cheveux = hair)*

> **FUN FACT:** In 1624 Louis XIII made the wig fashionable when he went bald and started to wear one. In the seventeenth century French nobles wore big curly wigs that flowed down their backs. Women wore white wigs and headdresses up to three feet high.

What do the French call the gentle **elbow** jab Napoléon sometimes gave his soldiers?

★ *His "***Coude*** Civil" (Code Civil = Civil Code; un coude = elbow)*

> **FUN FACT:** Napoléon's Civil Code gave France its first set of uniform laws. The Code had 2,281 articles defining laws about property, marriage, divorce, mortgages, wills, contracts, family law, and education.

What French day of the week is dedicated to the **belly**?

★ **ventre**-*di (vendredi; le ventre = belly)*

> **FUN FACT:** Louis XIV's stomach had twice the normal capacity. For each meal course he had a dozen choices. A princess once saw him eat four bowls of soup, a pheasant, a partridge, a large salad, two pieces of ham, mutton, and finally some cakes for dessert. Pass the Pepto-Bismol, please!

What do two people with a hotel reservation who share a **cold** have?

★ *a* **rhume** *for two (room; un rhume = cold)*

What do French **ear** specialists eat for snacks?

★ *Oreille-os and milk (Oreos; une oreille = ear)*

   FUN FACT: "Un oreiller" is a pillow. "Les oreillons" means "mumps."

What do French people do when they accidentally bump into someone with their **shoulder**?

★ *They épaule-ogize. (apologize; une épaule = shoulder)*

What do the French call it when someone takes the words right out of your **mouth**?

★ *being am-bouched (ambushed; la bouche = mouth)*

   FUN FACT: The French expression "Bouche cousue" (sewn mouth) means "It's a secret," "Mum's the word," or "Don't tell." A "bouche de métro" is a Paris subway entrance.

What French actress was **nose** to nose with King Kong when he picked her up?

★ *Nez-omi Watts (Naomi; un nez = nose)*

The tomb of what French **head** of state was recently discovered in Egypt?

★ *King Tête (Tut; une tête = head)*

Where in Europe do French manicurists go to learn how to paint **nail**s?

★ *They go to Ongle-terre. (Angleterre = England; un ongle = nail)*

What French film critic of the sea gave *Finding Nemo* eight **thumbs** up?

★ *an octo-**pouce*** *(octopus; un pouce = thumb)*

The Octo-pouce movie critic gives it eight thumbs up!

What did the French optometrist say when he sank a three-point basket to win the game?

★ *"Who's **yeux** Daddy!"* *(your; les yeux = eyes)*

FUN FACT: The French expression "les yeux plus gros que le ventre" means "your eyes are bigger than your stomach."

What brand of taco shells do French podiatrists buy?

★ ***Orteil**-ga* *(Ortega; un orteil = toe)*

What French pasta dish applauds when you serve it?

★ ***mains**-caroni and cheese* *(macaroni; une main = hand)*

What did one French rollerblader's **knee** say to the other knee?

⋆ *"Hey, where's **genou** knee pad?"* (your new; un genou = knee)

FUN FACT: Up to twenty thousand rollerbladers cruise around Paris on Sunday afternoons throughout the summer. The event is called a "rando roller" (rando, randonnée = excursion, hike).

Who do the French Munchkins call when they break a **bone**?

⋆ *the Wizard of **Os*** (Oz; un os = bone)

What music is played in French gyms when people are doing **leg** curls?

⋆ *jock **jambe**s* (jams; une jambe = leg)

Who wears a badge and protects French people's right to have **smooth skin**?

⋆ *the **peau-lisse*** (police; la peau = skin; lisse = smooth)

What did a hip hoppin' Elmer Fudd say to the French girl who was making a big scene and wagging her **finger** in his face?

⋆ *"Save the **doigt**-ma fo yo Mama."* (drama; un doigt = finger)

FUN FACT: In France students raise their pointing fingers to answer or ask questions while U.S. students raise their hands. A teacher says, "Levez le doigt." (Raise your finger.)

Where did the French mad scientist buy the feet for his monster, Frankenstein?

★ *at a **Pied**-Less Shoe Store* (Payless; un pied = foot)

FUN FACT: Add thirty-one to your shoe size to get your size in France.

What disease swept across France during the Middle Ages and made everyone grow **beard**s?

★ *the **Barbe**-onic Plague* (Bubonic; une barbe = beard)

FUN FACT: Cotton candy in French is "barbe à papa" or "Daddy's beard."

What do the three French musketeers proclaim when they all have **cough**s?

★ *"**Tousse** pour un, et un pour tousse."* (tous = all; [il] tousse = he coughs; Tous pour un et un pour tous = One for all, and all for one.)

CALENDAR AND CELEBRATIONS

Le calendrier et Les fêtes

Why do French people mow the grass on **Monday**?

★ Because it's **lawn**-di. *(lundi = Monday)*

FUN FACT: The French week and calendar begin on Monday, not Sunday.

What word best describes extroverted French people born in **August**?

★ very **août**-going *(outgoing; août = August)*

On what day does the French Snow White say her boyfriend will arrive?

★ "**Samedi**, *my prince will come.*" *(Someday; samedi = Saturday)*

> **FUN FACT:** Snow White is "Blanche Neige" in France. The seven dwarfs are the "sept nains."

What is a French **tuna** fish's favorite season?

★ *le prin-***thon** *(le printemps = spring; le thon = tuna)*

What do you get when you cross Miss Piggy and a page from a French calendar?

★ "**Mois?**" *("Moi?" un mois = month)*

What do French *Star Wars* fans call it when **Thursday** comes again?

★ *the return of the* **jeudi** *(The Return of the Jedi; jeudi = Thursday)*

Which French season weighs the most?

★ *l'au-***tonne** *(l'automne = autumn; une tonne = ton)*

What do French women call the new look they get every spring?

★ *a* **mai**-*kover (mai = May)*

What brand of flashlight batteries do French people use in the **winter**?

★ ***Hiver**-ready (Eveready; l'hiver = winter)*

When French people decorate their homes in the summer, what Chinese approach do they use?

★ *Feng **juillet** (feng shui; juillet = July)*

> **FUN FACT:** "Le 14 juillet," or the "Fête de la Bastille," is the French national holiday. It's celebrated with a military parade and fireworks set to music at the Eiffel Tower.

On what day do the French buy their fresh fish?

★ *on mackerel-di (mercredi = Wednesday)*

What does a French pessimist say is going to happen in **April**?

★ *"Nothing **avril** importance." (of real; avril = April)*

What do the French call the rules for proper social behavior in the **summer**?

★ ***Été**-quette (l'étiquette = rules of social behavior; l'été = summer)*

> **FUN FACT:** "Étiquettes" (tickets) were invitations to events held by Louis XIV with rules of behavior on them or signs with court rules posted around Versailles Palace.

What day of the French week always asserts itself?

★ ***jeudi***, *because it says* ***"je dis!"*** *(jeudi = Thursday; je dis = I say, tell)*

Why are French kangaroos born in **March**?

★ *Because they are **mars**-upials. (marsupials; mars = March)*

Which French airline can fly you to your destination **yesterday**?

★ ***Hier*** *France (Air France; hier = yesterday)*

Hier France—the only airline that gets you there . . . yesterday.

What chocolate candy bar is eaten in **March** in France?

★ *a **Mars** bar (mars = March)*

On which day of the week do French stores sell the most?

★ on **vendre**-di *(vendredi = Friday; vendre = to sell)*

What little pastel-colored candies that come in rolls do French children eat on **Tuesday**s?

★ S-**mardi**-es *(Smarties; mardi = Tuesday)*

What song from the musical *South Pacific* is sung each **week** in France?

★ "**Semaine** Enchanted Evening" *(Some; une semaine = week)*

On what day do French children play games?

★ on **jeux**-di *(jeudi = Thursday; des jeux = games)*

FUN FACT: William the Conqueror instituted a law that forbade any violence to occur on Mondays, Tuesdays, Thursdays, and Fridays.

What do you call a French person who's sick and tired of **holiday**s?

★ **Fête** up *(Fed; une fête = holiday, festival)*

FUN FACT: France has annual cultural festivals like: the Fête de Musique, Fête d'Internet, Fête de Pain (bread), the Lire en Fête (reading), and the Fête du Cinéma.

What kind of pasta do French people eat on **holiday**s?

★ **fête**-uccine *(fettuccine; une fête = holiday)*

Why is a **party** in France a real blast?

★ Because it's a **boum**! *(boom; une boum = party)*

> **FUN FACT:** A wealthy host once rented a section of the underground Paris Catacombs—filled with piles of neatly arranged skulls, tibias, and ulnas—for a party.

Why did the French woman party for twenty-four hours on November 1?

★ She wanted to get her **Toussaint**'s worth. *(two cents'; La Toussaint = All Saints' Day)*

> **FUN FACT:** On "La Toussaint" saints are commemorated. People visit grave sites of loved ones and leave chrysanthemums. Students get the week off from school.

What do the French think of Silly String?

★ They think it's da **bombe**. *(da bomb; une bombe = aerosol spray)*

What do you get when you cross a Montreal Canadien and the **Easter** bunny?

★ a hockey **Pâques** *(puck; Pâques = Easter)*

> **FUN FACT:** At Easter, candy shops in France have chocolate in many impressively large shapes such as decorated eggs, rabbits, soccer balls, and violins.

What do the French call giving a birthday **card** first and a teddy **bear** second?

★ *putting the **carte** before the **ours*** *(cart; horse; une carte = card; un ours = bear)*

How do French monkeys greet each other on New Year's Day?

★ *"Banane-née!"* *("Bonne année!" = "Happy New Year!")*

FUN FACT: On New Year's Eve in France, people kiss under mistletoe. They have a big meal called "Le Réveillon," exchange gifts, and sometimes go to dances.

On what national French holiday do people throw Polish sausages at each other?

★ *on Kilbasa-tille Day* *(Bastille Day = French national holiday, July 14)*

FUN FACT: The Bastille prison was attacked by Parisians on July 14, 1789, the beginning of the French Revolution. There were only seven prisoners there at the time.

What do French ghosts say when they step in **mud**?

★ *"Boue!"* *("Boo!"; la boue = mud)*

FUN FACT: Halloween has only been celebrated in France since 1996. The press and TV had to teach children and adults how to trick-or-treat.

Who bakes cookies and biscuits in France for all-occasion gift boxes?

★ the Pillsbury **Cadeaux** Boy *(Dough; des cadeaux = presents, gifts)*

What do the French call a fireworks display sponsored by Old Navy?

★ a **feu** d'artifleece *(feu d'artifice = fireworks display)*

What French holiday is dedicated to things that come in **two**'s?

★ the Fête des **paires** *(Fête des pères = Father's Day; des paires = pairs)*

FUN FACT: The French Father's Day is the third Sunday in June. "Heureuse fête des Pères!" ("Happy Father's Day!") "Bonne fête, Papa!" ("Happy Father's Day, Dad!")

What do the French call a successful **holiday** celebration?

★ a **fête** accompli *(fait accompli = accomplished act or done deal; une fête = holiday, celebration)*

What kind of healthy foods do French people eat on **holiday**s?

★ **fête** free *(fat free; une fête = holiday)*

What French holiday is dedicated to **beverages**?

★ **Boissons** *d'avril (Poisson d'avril = All Fool's Day, April 1; des boissons = beverages)*

> **FUN FACT:** In the sixteenth century New Year's was celebrated on April 1. When All Fool's Day replaced it, people got confused. Pranks were played on the "April Fools." Today French children stick paper fish on classmates' backs and stores sell chocolate fish.

What French holiday is dedicated to dirty clothes?

★ *the Jour de laundry (le Jour de l'An = New Year's Day)*

> **FUN FACT:** In France people send cards or e-mail greetings in January to wish each other health, happiness, and prosperity in the new year.

When do French people hang crêpes from the crystal lighting fixtures on their dining room ceilings?

★ *on Le Chandelier (La Chandeleur = a day when crêpes are made; February 2)*

> **FUN FACT:** "La Chandeleur" is a day about candles, crêpes, and good luck. A legend says if you flip six crêpes in a row, you'll find your special someone that year.

CRAZY

★

C'est fou!
(Très "goofé"!)

Which part of a Gothic French cathedral is sticky?

★ *a gargooey (une gargouille = gargoyle)*

FUN FACT: Gargoyles are confused with "chimères." A gargoyle juts out horizontally from a gutter and is used for water drainage. "Chimères" are the larger, more familiar demonic stone creatures that sit on top of cathedrals, guarding them from evil forces.

What French bubble gum makes people want to **kiss**?

★ **Bisou**-*ka (Bazooka; un bisou = kiss)*

FUN FACT: When French people see relatives or friends, they kiss each other on the cheeks with either two or four alternating kisses.

What is the name of the big green president of France who has a donkey sidekick?

★ *Jacques Shrek (Jacques Chirac = president of France)*

> **FUN FACT:** Jacques Chirac (1932–) was elected in 1995 and is in his second seven-year term. He was mayor of Paris from 1977 to 1995. Président Chirac is a big fan of sumo wrestling and of Japan. He has traveled to Japan over fifty times.

What is the name of the French fortune-telling board that always answers "Yes"?

★ *The **Oui**-ja board (Ouija; oui = yes)*

> **FUN FACT:** In 1853 a Frenchman named M. Planchette invented a table to predict the future. He sold it to an American who created the Ouija board.

What sport do they play in Dijon with a small paddle and a little seedless fruit?

★ *Grape Ping-Pong (Grey Poupon = brand of mustard from Dijon, France)*

> **FUN FACT:** Gustave Eiffel's family was in the mustard business. Because Eiffel wanted to build things and couldn't do so with mustard, he became an engineer and built bridges and towers.

What do French bakers study at cooking school?

★ ***farine** languages (foreign; la farine = flour)*

What do students at the French cooking school sing when their dishes flop?

★ *the cordon blues (École Cordon Bleu = Paris cooking school)*

FUN FACT: The École Cordon Bleu, founded in 1895, has twenty-six schools in fifteen countries around the world and attracts students to Paris from seventy countries.

What sound does a **rubber** French train make?

★ *"**Caoutchouc** choo!" ("Choo choo!"; le caoutchouc = rubber)*

What is a makeover for a French **queen** called?

★ *a **reine**-ovation (renovation; une reine = queen)*

What do romantic French **egg** vendors say about their language?

★ *It's the language of l'**œuf**. (love; un œuf = egg)*

What French headmaster of Hogwarts School of Wizardry and Witchcraft sleeps a lot?

★ *Albus Dumbledort (Dumbledore; [il] dort = [he] is sleeping)*

In which math class do French dogs communicate what x equals by barking?

★ *alg-aboie class (algebra; [il] aboie = [he] barks; aboyer = to bark)*

What is an attempt to overthrow a French pastry shop called?

★ *a coup des tartes* (coup d'état = overthrow of a government; des tartes = fruit tarts, small cakes)

What distinguished institution monitors the purity of French cats' meows?

★ *the A-cat-émie française* (Académie française)

FUN FACT: The Académie française was founded by Cardinal Richelieu in 1635. It monitors the vocabulary and use of the French language.

What kind of face cream do French women use?

★ *Oil of Oh Là Là Lay* (Oil of Olay; oh là là = wow)

Where does Garfield stay when he visits France?

★ *in a hotel cat étoiles* (hôtel quatre étoiles = four-star hotel)

What does a French plumber exclaim in frustration when he can't fix the toilet?

★ *"Ras le bowl."* (ras le bol = I'm fed up, I've had it up to here.)

What is a person who pretends to come from a French-speaking country called?

★ *a franco-phoney* (la francophonie = French-speaking world)

What two French verb forms for "I" are put on toast?

★ *J'aime* and *je lis* *(jam and jelly; j'aime = I like; je lis = I read)*

FUN FACT: "Bonne Maman" is a jam from France that is sold in the United States. The lids are checkered with white and red, purple, or blue.

Who was the first French queen to have her own website?

★ *Marie Internet (Marie Antoinette = Austrian-born queen of France)*

FUN FACT: Marie Antoinette (1755–1793) became the wife of Louis XIV and the queen of France when she was fourteen. She liked to go to masked balls and "play peasant" with her children at her little hamlet with a pond in the woods of Versailles.

Marie Internet was the first French queen to have her own website.

What happens every morning when a French amusement park opens?

★ **Foules** rush in. *(fools; une foule = crowd)*

> **FUN FACT:** The Parc Astérix north of Paris is an amusement park based on Astérix the comic book character and his friends. The park has a village of Gaul and life-size characters.

What is the name of the hair salon on top of Montmartre?

★ *Sacré-Curl (Sacré-Cœur)*

> **FUN FACT:** Sacré-Cœur is the white-domed basilica on top of the hill of Montmartre. The highest point in Paris is not on top of the Eiffel Tower, but at the observation point at the top of the Sacré-Cœur dome.

What is the study of unexplained mysterious events in the capital of France?

★ *Paris-psychology (parapsychology; la parapsychologie = parapsychology)*

How do French nannies greet each other?

★ *"What's* **nounou***?" (new; un nounou = nanny)*

What do you get when you cross an ice cream beverage and the attack of a king in French chess?

★ *a milk* **échec** *(milk shake; échec = check)*

Where in Mexico do the dancers from the Folies Bergère go for their vacations?

★ to **Cancan**-cun *(cancan = French cabaret dance)*

What did the French king shout to begin the **dance**s at his court?

★ *"Palais **bal**!"* *("Play ball!"; un bal = dance)*

What did Tina Turner ask when the chef at the École Cordon Bleu told her to put an **egg** in her sauce?

★ *"What's l'**œuf** got to do with it?"* *(love; un œuf = egg)*

When French and American cows call each other, what language do they speak?

★ *franglait (le franglais = words mixing French and English; le lait = milk)*

FUN FACT: "Franglais" comes from language mistakes; mixing words, or borrowing words like "un best-seller," "un thriller," "un skateboard."

What do you call an unmarried French woman who sells devices that allow computers to receive and transmit data over telephone or cable lines?

★ *a Modemoiselle (modem; mademoiselle = Miss, unmarried lady)*

FUN FACT: Mademoiselle is from "ma demoiselle" or "my young lady." It's used with a last name (Mademoiselle Martin) or both names (Mademoiselle Mimi Martin).

What did the French Terminator say when he failed his **high school exit exam**?

★ *"I'll be **bac**."* (back; le bac [baccalauréat] = French high school exit exam)

> **FUN FACT:** College-bound students spend their whole last year (terminale) studying for the "bac" exam. The test has a week of orals and essay writing and is taken in June.

The French Terminator fails his high school exit exam.

How often do French students use a **ruler**?

★ *on a **règle** basis* (regular; une règle = ruler)

What did the French girl testify under oath that she bought to hold her pencils and pens?

★ *"Deux **trousses** and nothing but deux **trousses**."* (truth; une trousse = pencil case)

How do reggae fans ask you if you speak **French**?

★ *"Marley-vous **français**?"* (Parlez; Parlez-vous français? = Do you speak French?)

What does Bart Simpson say about the stem of a French infinitive?

★ **"Radical**, Dude." (un radical = verb stem you get when you take the "-er," "-ir," or "-re" off a French infinitive)

FUN FACT: Bart once wrote this on a French blackboard: "La perruque du proviseur n'est pas un Frisbee." (The principal's wig is not a Frisbee.)

What toaster pastries does the **pope** eat for breakfast when he's in France?

★ **Pape**-Tartes (Pop-Tarts; un pape = pope)

What hobbit from Middle Earth searched for a ring and ended up ringing bells at Notre-Dame Cathedral in Paris?

★ *Quasifrodo* (Quasimodo; Frodo Baggins from The Lord of the Rings)

What do the French call teaching people how to play **checkers**?

★ **dames**-esticating them (domesticating; les dames = checkers)

What is the most **polite** French board game?

★ *Mono-**poli*** *(Monopoly; poli = polite)*

What did the French chickens' soccer team win in 1998?

★ *the Coop du Monde* *(Coupe du Monde = World Cup)*

What marketing slogan do you get when you cross
Coca-Cola with a brand of French beauty products?

★ *"It's **L'Oréal** thing."* *("It's the real thing.")*

What does a French cookie answer when asked,
"Ça va?"

★ *"Crumb si, crumb ça."* *(Comme si, comme ça = so-so; Ça va? =
How's it going?)*

To what social class do French cows belong?

★ *the moo-geoisie* *(la bourgeoisie = French middle class)*

How do **stylish** romantic French couples dance?

★ ***chic**-to-chic* *(cheek-to-cheek; chic = stylish, elegant)*

What is an attempt by French children to take over a
day-care center?

★ *a **coup** des tots* *(coup d'état = an attempt to take over a
government)*

What do French practical jokers say as they leave each other?

★ *"May the **farce** be with you."* (force; une farce = practical joke)

FUN FACT: Louis XIV once turned on a faucet and splashed guests who were visiting an underground tunnel at Versailles. He liked pranks.

What is a French comedian's Internet journal full of **joke**s called?

★ *a **blague*** (blog; une blague = joke)

Why couldn't the confused French carpenter hammer?

★ *He didn't have a **clou**.* (clue; un clou = nail)

Where do French tourists get the best view of Paris?

★ *on top of the Eyeful Tower* (Eiffel Tower)

How did the French lady duck describe her date?

★ *"He has a certain je ne sais coin about him."* (je ne sais quoi = I don't know what, an indefinable quality; Coin! = Quack!)

What do the French call the best Halloween treat in the bag?

★ *the pièce de Reese's-stance* (la pièce de résistance = main item in a series)

What do the French call the soft clay made with liver that children use to make imprints of comics?

★ *Silly **Pâté*** *(Silly Putty; le pâté = goose-liver spread)*

What do the French call the sheer thrill of using paper towels?

★ *the joie de Viva* *(joie de vivre = joy of living; Viva paper towels)*

What French company makes cake mixes and hats?

★ *Pills-**béret*** *(Pillsbury; un béret = classic French black or navy-blue wool cap)*

In what French movie does Tom Cruise have a difficult time trying to find a tire for his car?

★ ***Michelin*** *Impossible* (Mission Impossible; *Michelin = French tire company*)

What parlor game do French film directors like to play at parties?

★ ***Truffaut*** *Consequences* (truth or; *François Truffaut = director, producer, actor*)

FUN FACT: François Truffaut (1932–1984) was a giant in French filmmaking. He made thirty films, including *Fahrenheit 451*. He had a part in Steven Spielberg's *Close Encounters of the Third Kind*.

What play do you get when you cross the film *Clueless* and the French writer, Molière?

★ *"What-avare!"* *("Whatever!";* L'Avare = *a play by Molière; un avare = miser)*

FUN FACT: Molière (1622–1673) is called the Shakespeare of France. Actors couldn't be buried on holy ground unless they repented before they died. Molière died suddenly and had to be buried secretly at night by a priest. His grave was dug deeper than the usual fourteen feet, which was considered the depth of sacred ground.

What is the favorite dessert of French fencing experts?

★ **escrime** *(ice cream; l'escrime = fencing)*

What would the legendary French mime be called if he suddenly burst?

★ *Marcel Morceaux (Marceau; les morceaux = pieces)*

FUN FACT: Marcel Marceau (1923–) is the world's greatest mime. His white-faced character is called Bip.

FAMILY

★

La famille

What did the French boy say when he saw photos of his parents, brothers, and sisters?

★ *"These people look very **famille**-liar."* (familiar; une famille = family)

What do the French call an abundance of **sister**s in a family?

★ *a **sœur**-plus* (surplus; une sœur = sister)

What French children's song is about a very athletic **brother**?

★ *"**Frère** Jock"* ("Frère Jacques"; un frère = brother)

What do you get when you cross a frozen entrée with a slim French **cousin**?

★ *a Lean **Cousine*** (Lean Cuisine; une cousine = female cousin)

How do two French **sons** talk?

★ **fils**-*to*-*fils* *(face-to-face; un fils = son)*

What relative do French families take with them on camping trips?

★ *une* **tante** *(tent; une tente = tent; une tante = aunt)*

> **FUN FACT:** A nickname for a French aunt is "Tatie" as in "Tatie Babette."

What is the favorite hobby of a French **daughter**?

★ *la photogra-***fille** *(photography; la photographie = photography; une fille = daughter, girl)*

> **FUN FACT:** Louis Daguerre (1787–1851) was a pioneer in photography. He created the daguerreotype, an early photograph that fixed an image on a copper plate.

What adjective describes a confused French **father**?

★ **père**-*plexed* *(perplexed; un père = father)*

What do you call a French **sister** who pouts if she doesn't win a game?

★ *a* **sœur** *loser (sore; une sœur = sister)*

Which French family member gets stuck doing all the ironing?

★ *a* **frère** *à repasser (un fer à repasser = iron; un frère = brother; repasser = to iron)*

What is the queasy feeling a French **mother** gets at a shopping center?

★ *mall de* **mère** *(mal de mer = seasickness; une mère = mother)*

Which French relative makes the fewest errors in language?

★ *the* **grammaire** *(grandma; la grand-mère = grandmother; la grammaire = grammar)*

FUN FACT: A French grandmother is called "Mamie" or "Mémé."

From what store do sweet little French **girl**s come?

★ *a con-***fille**-*serie (une confiserie = candy store; une fille = girl)*

FUN FACT: Haribo marshmallow and gummi candies are sold in France. They come in shapes like French fries, snails, bananas, Coke bottles, burgers, crocodiles, alphabet letters, techno bears, pasta, bricks, cotton candy, and rattlesnakes.

In which American state do French **uncle**s spend their vacations?

★ *in* **Oncle**-*homa (Oklahoma; un oncle = uncle)*

FUN FACT: The nickname for a French uncle is "Tonton" as in "Tonton Georges."

In what car race does a French **niece** compete?

★ *a* **Nièce**-*car race (NASCAR; une nièce = niece)*

What do the French call it when a **wife** drops a ball?

★ *a **femme**-ble (fumble; une femme = wife, woman)*

What do the French call a **husband** who plays the trumpet in a Mexican band?

★ *a **mari**-achi (mariachi; un mari = husband)*

Which French relatives are **hilarious**?

★ *the grands-**marrants** (grandparents; les grands-parents = grandparents; marrant[s] = hilarious)*

What is the favorite Caribbean dance of a French **mother**?

★ *the **mère**-engue (merengue; une mère = mother)*

What is a French **niece**'s favorite coffee?

★ ***Nièce**-café (Nescafé; une nièce = niece)*

According to Peter Pan, where do French **nephew**s live forever?

★ *in **Neveu** Neveu Land (Never; un neveu = nephew)*

What can you say about a French **daughter-in-law** who's a little crazy?

★ *There are bats in the **belle-fille**. (belfry; une belle-fille = daughter-in-law)*

What family member has a colorful and explosive
personality?

✱ *a feu d'arti-fils* (*un feu d'artifice = fireworks display; un fils =
son*)

What kind of car does a French **brother** drive?

✱ *a **Frère**-ari* (*Ferrari; un frère = brother*)

Which French relatives love to ride the suburban Paris
trains?

✱ *the RER grands-parents* (*arrière-grands-parents = great-
grandparents; RER = train system of Paris and its suburbs*)

FASHION

★

La mode, oh Là Là!

During which elegant era in Paris did blouses and pants expose the tummy?

★ *the Belly-poque (la Belle Époque)*

FUN FACT: The Belle Époque (beautiful era) was a time of prosperity and luxury in France, between 1880 and 1914. Scientific advances dazzled the public. Photography, the cinema, and bicycles were invented and the Eiffel Tower was built. Parisians strolled the wide grand boulevards in their finest clothing, jewelry, and hats and were entertained by shows, amusements, and shopping.

How does a French **coat** know you're going to buy it?

★ *It has **manteau** telepathy. (mental; un manteau = coat)*

What state is dedicated to French **socks**?

★ *Massa-**chaussettes** (Massachusetts; les chaussettes = socks)*

What word describes a cute French girl in a dress by designer Christian?

★ a-**Dior**-able *(adorable; Christian Dior)*

FUN FACT: Christian Dior (1905–1957) was an international leader in design who helped make Paris the fashion capital of the world. His assistant was Yves St. Laurent. Dior makes J'Adore and Poison perfumes and the men's cologne Fahrenheit.

What wizard from Middle Earth has long gray hair, a gray beard, and wears hot-pink silk **gloves**?

★ **Gants**-dalf *(Gandalf; les gants = gloves)*

What French cologne does Jim Carrey wear in the film in which he tells fibs?

★ *Liar Liar du Temps* *(L'Air du Temps = French perfume by Nina Ricci; Liar Liar)*

FUN FACT: Napoléon really liked a cologne that was made with violets. He splashed eight quarts of it on himself each month.

What is the favorite sandwich of people who manufacture French **vests**?

★ *Peanut butter and* **gilet** *(jelly; un gilet = vest, cardigan)*

FUN FACT: Peanut butter is hard to find in France. It isn't that popular. Nutella, a chocolate-hazelnut spread, is very popular on bread and crêpes, though. It's also sold in the United States.

What toast is heard at Paris cafés when **fashion** designers raise their glasses?

✦ *"Here's **mode** in your eye."* *(mud; la mode = fashion, style)*

> **FUN FACT:** Four fashion phrases are: "à la mode" (in style), "démodé" (out of style), "lancer une mode" (set a style, trend), and "être à la mode" (to be in style).

What French fashion style has tropical birds sitting on people's shoulders?

✦ *parrot-à-porter* *(prêt-à-porter = ready-to-wear clothes; porter = to wear)*

> **FUN FACT:** Paris fashions used to be custom made (couture) for the wealthy. In the twentieth century, designers began mass-producing ready-to-wear fashions. They came in many sizes and colors and were available to the public. "Vive le shopping!"

The latest fashion trend hits Paris—parrot-à-porter.

What do you call the supports some French women put on their high-heeled **boot**s?

★ flying **botte**-tresses *(buttresses; une botte = boot)*

FUN FACT: Flying buttresses are the winglike supports that run along both sides of French Gothic cathedrals. They support the weight of the massive walls, allowing cathedrals to reach great heights and stained-glass windows to be added.

What article of clothing distributes the weight of a French person?

★ *The belt, because it's the* **ceinture** *of gravity. (center; une ceinture = belt)*

Why can you tell your secrets to French **lace** makers?

★ *Because they* **dentelle**. *(don't tell; la dentelle = lace)*

What kind of person is a French **fabric** designer?

★ **étoffe** *guy (a tough; une étoffe = fabric)*

FUN FACT: The best district in Paris with a great selection of eye-dazzling fabrics is an area on Montmartre at the base of the Sacré-Cœur stairs around Saint-Pierre Square.

What did the Paris jeweler say when describing her new boyfriend?

★ *"He's all that and a* **bague** *of diamond chips!" (all that and a bag of chips!; une bague = ring)*

Who wears a mask, rides a horse, rights injustices, and sells **pants** in Paris?

★ The **Pantalon** Ranger *(Lone Ranger; un pantalon = pair of pants)*

What do you call a French woman who is obsessed with buying **hat**s?

★ a **chapeau**-holic *(shopoholic; un chapeau = hat)*

> **FUN FACT:** Napoléon's hat is called a "bicorne." It had a blue, white, and red "cocarde," or rosette, on it.

"I'm a chapeau-holic!"

What did Hamlet shout when he spotted the perfect **dress** for his mother in Paris?

★ "Ay, there's the **robe**!" *(rub [from a Hamlet soliloquy]; une robe = dress)*

What do French fashion designers order for dinner in restaurants?

★ *des **filets*** *(un défilé = parade, fashion show; un filet = steak)*

FUN FACT: A "filet" in French is a piece of boneless steak or fish, just as it is in English. It's also a net or a netted bag that people take with them to the market.

What fragrance do French women wear on summer evenings?

★ *Eau de Twilight* *(eau de toilette = scented water)*

FUN FACT: "Toilette" in French means one's daily grooming. In seventeenth-century France there was no plumbing and bathing was rare, so scented oils and extracts were put into sponge-bath water. The perfume and toiletries industry was born. Twilight in France in the summer makes it stay light in the evenings until 9:30 P.M. or later.

Can a **model** make a lot of money in Paris?

★ ***Mannequin** and many can't.* *(many can; un mannequin = model)*

Who visits French children at night when they put a **slipper** under their pillows?

★ *the **pantoufle** fairy* *(tooth; une pantoufle = slipper)*

FUN FACT: An error was made when Charles Perrault's French version of *Cinderella* was translated. "Pantoufles en vair," or fur slippers, was translated "pantoufles en verre," which means "glass slippers." "Vair" and "verre" sound alike.

When the French inventor of a stretch body garment worn by ballet dancers was late to school, what did his teacher say?

★ *"Léo, tardy!"* *(un léotard = leotard; Jules Léotard = world's first trapeze artist)*

FUN FACT: Jules Léotard (1839–1870) invented the leotard worn by acrobats, gymnasts, and ballet dancers. Léotard inspired "The Daring Young Man on the Flying Trapeze." If he had a partner named Annette, he would have been working without Annette when she was sick. (Groan!)

What is the cross between the life of a French fashion model and an Édith Piaf hit?

★ *"La Vie en pose"* *("La Vie en rose" = Piaf hit)*

FUN FACT: "La Vie en rose" is looking at life through rose-colored glasses, not realistically. The singer Édith Piaf apparently wrote the song but never got the copyright to the international hit.

What does a grouchy French **ring** salesman say around the holidays?

★ *"Bah, ham-**bague**."* *(humbug; une bague = ring)*

What disease do French polka-dot **shirt**s get?

★ the **chemise**-als *(measles; une chemise = shirt, blouse)*

For what national raffle do French people buy tickets and hope to win **underwear**?

★ the **culotte**-ery *(lottery; une culotte = underwear, briefs)*

What do French teenagers wear on their heads that allows them to film?

★ a vidéo-**casquette** *(une casquette = cap; une vidéo-cassette = videocassette)*

Why did the French **shoe** salesman decide not to open his own store?

★ He wasn't **chaussure** of himself. *(so sure; une chaussure = shoe)*

FUN FACT: The French king Charles VIII started a fashion trend. Because he had six toes on one foot, he had to wear wide squared-off shoes. Soon everyone across Europe had to have a pair.

What did the French teenager say when she saw the gorgeous **bathing suit**?

★ "**Maillot** my!" *("My, oh, my!"; un maillot (de bain) = bathing suit)*

FUN FACT: The "maillot jaune" (yellow jersey) is awarded to the winner of each day's leg of the Tour de France bike race. That winner gets to wear it the following day.

What do the French call a flattering comment about a **suit**?

★ *a **complet**-ment (compliment; un complet = suit)*

What does a French **fabric** vendor use to blow his nose?

★ *a **tissu** (tissue; un tissu = fabric)*

What does the French Santa wear when he and his reindeer take a ride on a sunny day?

★ *his **lunettes** de sleigh (les lunettes de soleil = sunglasses)*

Why do French **suspenders** crack easily?

★ *Because they are very **bretelles**. (brittle; les bretelles = suspenders)*

What kind of beef does a French jeweler order at a restaurant?

★ *roast beef au **bijoux** (au jus; les bijoux = jewelry)*

What article of French clothing is like a smart citrus fruit?

★ ***écharpe orange** (a sharp orange; une écharpe orange = orange scarf)*

FRANCE

★

Vive La France!

What do you consult to learn about things that are French?

★ *a re-**France** book (reference; France)*

FUN FACT: The French invented the smart card, metric system, Aqua-Lung, bicycle, Braille, gyroscope, pencil, mayonnaise, diesel engine, bikini, calculator, parachute, sewing machine, HDTV, perfume, fiber optics, pasteurization, tuxedo, seaplane, hot air balloon, stethoscope, ambulance, cinema, and photography.

What do you call the distance around the country whose capital is Paris?

★ *the circum-**France** (circumference)*

FUN FACT: France is called the "Hexagone" (hexagon) because it has six sides. France is about twice the size of Colorado or four-fifths the size of Texas.

Who lost her sheep in a northern French textile city?

★ **Lille** Bo Beep *(Little; Lille = industrial city of northern France)*

FUN FACT: Lille has only been part of France for three hundred years. Its public transportation system called Lille Val has automatic cars that run without drivers.

What French TV show is about alien investigations in a small town in Provence?

★ The *"Aix-Files"* *("The X-Files"; Aix-en-Provence [called just "Aix," for short])*

FUN FACT: Aix-en-Provence is located in Provence. It was built on an area of hot springs in 123 B.C. by the Romans and is referred to as the city of a thousand fountains.

According to archaeologists from Brittany, what's the opposite of loving someone from afar?

★ loving someone from **menhir** *(a near; un menhir = large prehistoric stone)*

FUN FACT: Menhirs are giant mysterious vertical stones in Brittany. One is thirty-one feet tall. There are three thousand menhirs in Brittany. Carnac has the largest number of them.

When do the people of Champagne add fabric softener to their laundry?

★ during the final **Reims** *(rinse; Reims = city in northern France)*

FUN FACT: Reims is in Champagne. French kings, from Clovis in 481 through Charles X in 1825, were crowned in Notre-Dame Cathedral of Reims.

What did Joan of Arc ask the English soldiers in a Normandy town before she was burned at the stake?

★ *"Why did you have to go and **Rouen** my day?"* (ruin; Rouen = capital of upper Normandy)

FUN FACT: Rouen is where Joan of Arc was burned at the stake by the English in 1431. She tried to escape and even jumped seventy feet from a tower, but her fate was sealed. In 1456 the Inquisition declared her innocent of the charges. Rouen was almost completely destroyed by bombing during World War II.

What does a resident of the French Riviera put on when it's cold?

★ *a coat d'azur* (la Côte d'Azur = coast of azur blue = French Riviera)

FUN FACT: The Côte d'Azur is on the Mediterranean Sea. Cannes, Nice, Saint-Tropez, Antibes, and the Principality of Monaco are on the Riviera. The sun is said to shine there more than three hundred days a year. Pass the Bain de Soleil, please!

What French TV show is about two women in the 1950s who work at a brewery in a region of central France?

★ *"**L'Auvergne** and Shirley"* ("Laverne and Shirley"; Auvergne = province in central France)

FUN FACT: Auvergne in central France has over eighty extinct volcanoes, hundreds of thermal springs, and tall thin volcanic needle rocks.

Where in France do Elvis impersonators live?

★ in **Grasse**-land *(Graceland; Grasse = town in Provence)*

FUN FACT: Grasse is the perfume center of France, producing two-thirds of the scents used in France's perfume industry. The Moors brought jasmine to Grasse in the sixteenth century, and the town produces twenty-seven tons of it each year.

What are two popular snacks of people from the northern French port of Dieppe?

★ chips and onion **Dieppe** and nine-layer **Dieppe** *(dip; Dieppe = French town)*

Who was the principal fashion designer at Louis XIV's royal palace?

★ **Versailles**-ce *(Versace; Versailles = palace built by Louis XIV)*

FUN FACT: Versailles Palace is ten miles from Paris and covers thirty square miles. It has 700 rooms, 1,250 fireplaces, 67 staircases, 120 miles of canals, 1,400 golden fountains, a 55-acre canal, and an orange grove. Louis liked fresh oranges.

What do you call the ability to get around the ski resorts of the French Alps?

★ **Savoie**-faire *(savoir-faire = know-how; Savoie = region in the French Alps)*

FUN FACT: Savoie has many ski resorts, alpine meadows, chalets, and even a glacier. Its major cities are Chamonix, Annecy, and Albertville, the site of the 1992 Winter Olympics.

What was the major brand of electronics used at a fortress in southwest France?

★ *Carcass-Sony* (Carcassonne = 2,000-year-old fortified city or château fort)

FUN FACT: When Pépin laid siege to the city, the people were starving. Dame Carcas had them feed all their grain to one pig, and the fattened pig was thrown over the walls. Pépin was tricked into thinking they had tons of food, and left. Dame Carcas rang the bells in victory. "Carcas sonne" means "(Dame) Carcas rings."

After her husband went to work, when did the French woman say she would make the whipped cream for dessert?

★ *"I chan't till he returns."* (shan't; Chantilly = a town thirty miles from Paris)

FUN FACT: The French chef Vatel created a variation of whipped cream for a special dessert for Louis XIV. It became known as "crème de Chantilly."

What do you get when you cross a Louis XIV dance and the body part used for sight?

★ *a **Versailles** ball* (Versailles ball; eyeball; Versailles Palace)

FUN FACT: The French invented the masked ball (bal masqué), which was common at Versailles. The nobles and courtiers dressed in costumes of characters from operas, plays, and literature. They wore wigs, makeup, and masks. Louis XIV liked to dance and required all his courtiers and the nobles to take dance lessons.

What did the French pear say as he started to leave for the Loire mall and saw his friend standing still?

★ "***Anjou** coming with me?*" *(Aren't you; Anjou = Loire Valley region)*

 FUN FACT: Anjou pears were introduced to the United States in 1842. They are in most supermarkets and have labels with "Anjou" on them.

What did the Grey Poupon man answer when Homer Simpson's son asked him if hens lay **eggs** in **Corsica**?

★ "*Bart, **œuf Corse!**"* *("But, of course!" un œuf = egg; la Corse = Corsica)*

 FUN FACT: Corsica is a mountainous island in the Mediterranean Sea that is part of France. Ajaccio is its capital. The island has two hundred beaches and thirty diving clubs. Corsica is the birthplace of Napoléon.

What did the French archaeologist say when his colleague asked him if he wanted to see some cave paintings?

★ "*Sure. **Lascaux!**"* *(Let's go; Lascaux = cave with prehistoric paintings)*

 FUN FACT: The Lascaux cave in southwestern France was discovered in 1940 by children playing in the woods. Their dog disappeared and when they found it, it was digging in the ground. The children began to dig, too, and discovered the cave.

What French city is the most musical?

★ *Do-re-mi* (Domrémy = a town in northeast France)

FUN FACT: Domrémy in the province of Lorraine in northeast France is the town where Joan of Arc was born. Her medieval home is still there.

What do philosophers from a northern French port have?

★ **Dieppe** *thoughts* (deep; Dieppe = French port)

FUN FACT: Dieppe is a port on the northern coast of France with ferries to England and elsewhere. Dieppe has an annual kite festival.

What gas station chain is seen along the roads of southeastern France?

★ *Exxon* **Provence** (Aix-en-Provence = former capital of Provence)

FUN FACT: Aix-en-Provence is called the Florence of Provence.

What French TV show is about apprehending criminals near France's longest river?

★ *"**Loire** and Order"* ("Law and Order"; Loire River = river that flows through Normandy)

FUN FACT: French kings and nobles built three hundred châteaux in the Loire Valley. Six famous ones are: Chambord, Chinon, Azay-le-Rideau, Chenonceau, Blois, and Amboise.

In which French city is there always a smile on everyone's face?

★ *Grin-oble* (Grenoble = *French city in the southern French Alps*)

FUN FACT: Grenoble is a center of science and research in the areas of math, computer science, atomic energy, chemistry, and physics. The University of Grenoble was founded in 1339.

What French ski resort is run by a famous Sea World whale?

★ *Shamu-nix* (Chamonix = *ski resort in the French Alps*)

FUN FACT: Chamonix, at the foot of Mont Blanc in the French Alps, has been a ski resort for two hundred years. It has thirty thousand acres with six ski areas and 145 trails.

What do surgeons on the French Riviera give their patients before operations?

★ *a-**Nice**-thesia* (anesthesia; Nice = *large city on the Riviera*)

FUN FACT: Nice was named after Nike, the goddess of victory. "Bouillabaisse," a fish soup, and the "salade niçoise," which has hard-boiled eggs and anchovies, are two specialties of Nice.

What do you get when you cross Granny Smiths and a northeastern French province?

★ *app-**Alsace*** (applesauce; Alsace = *region in northeast France*)

FUN FACT: The capital of Alsace is Strasbourg. Alsace is famous for sauerkraut, gingerbread, and flaming tarts that are like oven-baked pizzas with fresh cream, onions, and bacon on them.

What is the favorite brand of ice cream of a synagogue leader from the Pyrenees?

⋆ **Basque 'n' Rabbins** *(Baskin-Robbins; un rabbin = rabbi; Basque = a person who lives in the Pyrenees mountains between France and Spain)*

FUN FACT: The origin of the Basques is a mystery because they are of neither French nor Spanish descent. The Basques gave the beret and the game of jai alai (pelota) to the world.

What kind of music do inhabitants of French châteaux like?

⋆ *Chenon-soul music (Chenonceaux = château in the Loire Valley)*

FUN FACT: Chenonceaux is a dreamy château in the Loire Valley that was built three times and once was a mill. It has a magnificent ballroom with a black-and-white checkered marble floor that extends behind the building and crosses a river like a bridge. Diane de Poitiers lived there for many years.

What do children in a northern coastal French town use to sculpt objects?

⋆ *modeling* **Calais** *(clay; Calais = northernmost town on the Atlantic)*

FUN FACT: Swimmers from forty-seven countries have battled the strong, frigid currents of the English Channel between Calais, France, and Dover, England, over 750 times. One woman swam the twenty-one miles more than thirty times.

What do the people of Normandy take for headaches?

★ ***Bayeux*** *aspirin (Bayer; Bayeux = Normandy town)*

> **FUN FACT:** Bayeux was the first French town liberated when the allies landed on the Normandy coast on D-Day in 1944. The Bayeux Tapestry shows scenes from the Battle of Hastings in 1066 when William the Conqueror invaded England.

What kind of car do people from France's largest Mediterranean port city drive?

★ *a **Marseille**-des (Mercedes; Marseille = second largest French city)*

> **FUN FACT:** Marseille is famous for its "Savon de Marseille," a soap made with olive oil or palm oil. The Château d'If, the former island prison made popular by Alexander Dumas in *The Count of Monte Cristo*, is off the coast of Marseille.

What do people from the Bordeaux region of France sing on New Year's Eve?

★ *"Should old **Aquitaines** be forgot . . . " (acquaintance; Aquitaine = region in southwest France)*

> **FUN FACT:** During the twelfth century, Aquitaine was ruled by Eleanor of Aquitaine who continued to expand her property. When she married Henry II of England, he took control, she rebelled, and he imprisoned her for fifteen years. When he died, she regained power. Eleanor lived to be eighty years old, which was a rare feat for the Middle Ages.

How do Paris tourists describe the city's boat cruise?

★ **"Seine**-sational." *(Seine = river that flows through Paris)*

FUN FACT: The "bateau-mouche" (fly-boat) ride is extra special—and romantic—in the evening. Tourists can see the sun set behind Paris monuments and watch as the City of Lights is illuminated.

What did the mayor of the World War II French capital say when bottles of mineral water began to mysteriously disappear?

★ "Something **Vichy**'s going on around here." *(fishy's; Vichy = French city)*

FUN FACT: Vichy has many mineral springs and is a resort town and spa. It was the seat of the French government between 1940 and 1944 when the Nazis occupied Paris and most of France.

What city on the coast of Brittany goes well with peanut butter?

★ *Saint-Marsh-mallow (marshmallow; Saint-Malo = walled city on the coast of Brittany)*

FUN FACT: Saint-Malo was a haven for pirates and corsairs who stole from pirates. Jacques Cartier was born there. At high tide, powerful waves can splash over the double walls of the city, so the townspeople keep schedules of the tides in their wallets to be safe.

What is a sneaky thief from the French Riviera called?

★ a **Cannes** man *(con man; Cannes = city on the French Riviera)*

FUN FACT: Cannes is a luxurious city of the wealthy. The Cannes Film Festival takes place there each May. Beverly Hills is its sister city. Elegant hotels, Mercedes and Jaguars, casinos, celebrities, yachts, surfing . . . oh, là là!

What are the favorite crackers of people who live in a French surfing city on the Atlantic?

★ *Biar-Ritz (Biarritz = resort on the southwest Basque coast)*

FUN FACT: Napoléon spent many summers at his Biarritz house. Surfing in France began in Biarritz. The city hosts an annual international surfing festival.

Who had to make 440 beds each day at the château of François I?

★ the **Chambord**-maid *(chambermaid; Chambord = largest château of the Loire Valley)*

FUN FACT: Chambord also has six wide towers, 365 fireplaces, and 84 staircases. Its roofs are topped with turrets, spires, dormers, and hundreds of chimneys. Tourists can walk on the roof.

What do people who live in the highest mountains of France feed their dogs?

★ *Alpe-au (Alpo; French Alps)*

FUN FACT: The highest mountain in the French Alps is Mont Blanc at 15,632 feet. There are more than 2,500 ski trails in the French Alps.

What can you say about the tourist who mistakenly went to Caen, Normandy, looking for the famous film festival?

★ *He got **Cannes**-fused. (confused; Cannes = city on the French Riviera)*

FUN FACT: Caen is pronounced "KUH" and Cannes is pronounced "KAHN."

What does a dentist from France's third largest city pull out of his patients' mouths and his lawn?

★ *dents de **Lyon** (des dents = teeth; Lyon = third largest French city; des dents de lion = lion's teeth = dandelions)*

FUN FACT: Lyon is known for its cuisine and chefs like Paul Bocuse. Lyonnaise potatoes are a local specialty. The Lumière brothers opened the world's first cinema there in 1895. The headquarters of INTERPOL, the international police, is in Lyon.

What city in the Loire Valley was named after the blue enemy of the Masters of the Universe comic book character, He-Man?

★ *Skele-**Tours** (Skeletor; Tours = capital of the château region)*

FUN FACT: Tours, on the quiet Loire River, is called the "garden of France." It was the cradle of the French Renaissance and is called the birthplace of the French language.

What do people of a French island abbey wear to keep track of the times of the tides?

★ a **Montre**-Saint-Michel *(Mont-Saint-Michel; une montre = watch)*

FUN FACT: Mont-Saint-Michel is a Benedictine abbey on a small island surrounded by water at high tide. Scientists say the tide comes in fifty feet deep at up to twelve miles per hour. Low tide leaves nine miles of eerie tidal flats that have dangerous quicksand.

What do you say to encourage a person who is thinking about applying for a job in France's city of aeronautics?

★ *"What have you got **Toulouse**?"* *(to lose; Toulouse = southeastern French city)*

FUN FACT: Toulouse is the "pink city" because of its brick architecture. The city, located on the Canal du Midi, is the center of the French aeronautics industry. The author of *Le Petit Prince*, Antoine de Saint-Exupéry, was born in Toulouse.

What do the people of Auvergne put on the volcanic needle rocks so they won't deteriorate?

★ a **puy**-servative *(preservative; un puy = tall volcanic needle)*

FUN FACT: A "puy" is a very tall, thin, pointed rock that looks like a needle. The tallest "puy" in central France is the Puy de Sancy. It is 6,184 feet high.

When the fisherman from Brittany didn't fix the leak in his boat and it sank, what did his friends say?

★ *"It's something you **Bretagne** yourself."* (brought on; Bretagne = French province known for its fishing industry)

FUN FACT: Bretagne (Brittany) is a province comprising the largest French peninsula in the Atlantic. Brittany's ancestors were Celts and the Celtic language is still spoken there. The crêpe originated in Brittany.

What is the beef patty capital of France?

★ *Hamburg-ogne* (Bourgogne = Burgundy, a province in western France)

FUN FACT: Bourgogne is famous for "bœuf bourguignon" (beef and vegetables) and "escargots" (snails). It has a 155-mile canal and barge tours. Dijon, the mustard capital, is in Bourgogne.

FRUITS AND VEGETABLES

★

Les fruits et Les Légumes

Which château is a cross between François I and a red berry?

★ **Framboise** *(Amboise = castle of François I; une framboise = raspberry)*

FUN FACT: François I lived at Amboise on the Loire River. He convinced Leonardo da Vinci to move to the village of Amboise. The artist spent the last years of his life there and is buried in a small chapel on the château grounds.

Where do the relatives of a French **apple** live?

★ in a **pomme** kin patch *(pumpkin; pomme = apple)*

What do French people purchase in case they are hit with a **cabbage**?

★ in-**chou**-rance *(insurance; un chou = cabbage)*

> **FUN FACT:** A "chouchou" is a teacher's pet. "Mon petit chou" means "my little pet" or "my darling." Other sweet terms are: "mon chéri" or "ma chérie" (my dear), "mon petit canard" (little duckling), "ma cocotte" (little hen), "mon coco" (little egg), and "ma puce" (flea).

I'm glad I have in-CHOU-rance!

French people are covered in case of accidents involving cabbages.

What is green and attends Hogwarts School of Witchcraft and Wizardry?

★ **Haricot** Potter *(Harry; un haricot = bean)*

What does a French **garlic** say when it gets married?

★ **"Ail** do." *("I do"; un ail = garlic)*

What do you get when you cross a French **potato** and a cheerleader?

⋆ *a pomme **pomme** de terre* (pom-pom; *une pomme de terre* = potato)

FUN FACT: In 1787 Antoine-Augustin Parmentier solved a famine problem by planting France's first potatoes in the Champ de Mars, which is today in the shadow of the Eiffel Tower.

What do French people put on a **radish** before eating it?

⋆ ***Radis** Whip* (Reddi-Whip; *un radis* = radish)

FUN FACT: "Je n'ai pas un radis" ("I don't have a radish") means "I'm broke." When radishes want to leave a party, they ask their friends, "Are you 'radis' to go?"

What did the flirtatious French **garlic** vendor tell the woman who came to his stand?

⋆ *"I only have **ail**s for you."* (eyes; *un ail* = garlic)

What do you call a French **blackberry** in a satin dress, diamonds, makeup, and a tiara?

⋆ *gla-**mûre**-ous* (glamorous; *une mûre* = blackberry)

What does a French **grape** philosopher contemplate?

⋆ *its **raisin** d'être* (*raison d'être* = reason for living, reason for existence; *un raisin* = grape)

Why did the French girl use a conditioner after getting hit in the head with a **strawberry**?

★ *to get rid of the **fraise** in her hair* (frizz; une fraise = strawberry)

What is said in the wedding ceremony of two French **plum**s just before they kiss?

★ *"I now **pruneau**-nce you man and wife."* (pronounce; un pruneau = plum)

What French music download gadget can give you bad breath?

★ *an **ail**-Pod* (iPod; un ail = garlic)

FUN FACT: Garlic gave Napoléon Bonaparte stomach pains. Once he ate some stew and didn't realize it had garlic in it. The next day he was so sick he thought he had been poisoned.

From where in the Middle East does France import **banana**s?

★ *from La-**banane*** (Lebanon; la banane = banana)

What do you call a private chat between two French **tomato**es?

★ *an in-**tomate** conversation* (intimate; une tomate = tomato)

What kind of denim pants do French eggplants wear?

★ *auber-jeans* (les aubergines = eggplants)

What is yellow and fuzzy and needed by French fruits to travel abroad?

⋆ a **pêche**-*port* (passport; une pêche = peach)

If you put a French **cabbage** at the end of one leg and you move it to the end of your other leg, what can you conclude?

⋆ The **chou**'s on the other foot. (shoe's; un chou = cabbage)

What do the French call Wheaties with **mushrooms**?

⋆ The Breakfast of **Champignons** (Champions; un champignon = mushroom)

What do the French call a detective movie with a plot that drives you **nuts**?

⋆ a film **noix** (film noir = black-and-white detective films of the 1940s; les noix = nuts)

FUN FACT: "Film noir" means "black cinema" or "black film" and refers to the dark detective, crime, gangster, and mystery movies of the 1940s to the 1960s in America. French critics coined the phrase.

What do you call a French **artichoke** that flexes his muscles in front of his girlfriend?

⋆ an **artichaut**-*off* (show-off; un artichaut = artichoke)

What kind of car do French people drive on Halloween?

⋆ a **Citrouille**-ën (Citroën = French car; une citrouille = pumpkin)

What do French women call a gloss that tastes like **watermelon**?

★ *lip* **pastèque** *(lipstick; la pastèque = watermelon)*

What **brown** French nut is really **hilarious**?

★ *a* **marron** *marron* **marrant** *(un marron = chestnut, brown; marrant = hilarious)*

What French salad ingredient prompts people to say "Gezundheit"?

★ *Lettuce, because it's "***laitue***."* *(a-choo; la laitue = lettuce)*

What does a French **turnip** soccer team need for the big game?

★ *a plan* **navet**-*tack (of attack; un navet = turnip)*

FUN FACT: Salvador Dali, the eccentric painter with a museum in Paris, once arrived at an event in a limo full of turnips. A "navet" is also a film that's a box-office flop.

What was the French **asparagus** doing when it spread gossip and rumors?

★ *It was casting* **asperge**-*ions. (aspersions; les asperges = asparagus)*

What do French TV chefs call a leftover **rice** dish that's served the next night?

★ *a* **riz**-*run (rerun; le riz = rice)*

HOUSE

★

La maison

What French website sells **house**s?

★ *Am-**maison**.com (Amazon.com; une maison = house)*

What must French people have a lot of if they want to buy a **palace**?

★ ***Palais** dough (Play-Doh; un palais = palace)*

What is the shape of a **roof** in France?

★ *a **toit**-pezoid (trapezoid; un toit = roof)*

What do French home owners sing when they have to mow the **lawn**?

★ *They sing the **pelouse**. (blues; la pelouse = lawn)*

In what dessert can French people sit?

★ a **chaise**-*cake* (cheesecake; une chaise = chair)

What friend of Hercules fights warlords and lives in a
French **kitchen**?

★ **Cuisine**-*na, Warrior Princess* (Xena; une cuisine = kitchen)

What cut of beef do French people eat in the **living
room**?

★ a **salon** *steak* (sirloin; un salon = living room)

What room in a French house do you get when you
cross a store clearance, a nut, and late-night host, Leno?

★ a *sale almond Jay* (une salle à manger = dining room)

What kind of hats do Mexican tourists wear in French
bedrooms?

★ **chambre**-*eros* (sombreros; une chambre = bedroom)

What pair of French explorers traveled along the
Mississippi selling **wall-to-wall carpeting**?

★ **Moquette** *and Joliet* (Marquette; la moquette = wall-to-wall
  carpeting)

  FUN FACT: In 1673 Jacques Marquette and Louis Joliet left
  Quebec and explored the Great Lakes, parts of Wisconsin and
  Illinois, and the Mississippi River. They were the first white men
  to see Missouri.

In which room of the house do French people eat **lettuce**?

★ *in the **salade** de bains (salle de bains = bathroom; la salade = lettuce)*

FUN FACT: Lettuce eaten alone with a dressing is called "la salade" and is common at French meals. The French "salle de bains" is for bathing only and does not have a toilet. The small room called "les toilettes" or "WC" (water closet) has a toilet and a sink.

Xavier is in the bathroom eating a "salade de bains."

What is the nationality of **door**s in France?

★ **Porte**-*uguese (Portuguese; une porte = door)*

FUN FACT: French doors are made of small panes of glass. They often come in pairs. French doors divide two rooms or open onto patios or gardens.

How many **window**s are there in France?

★ *an in-**fenêtre** number* (infinite; une fenêtre = window)

What sound does a French **wall** make?

★ *a **mur**mur* (un mur = wall)

FUN FACT: "Les murs ont des oreilles" means "the walls have ears."

What does a French woman say when she finds out she's getting a new **oven**?

★ *"**Four** real?"* (for; un four = oven)

FUN FACT: In early France before homes had ovens, there was one oven in the center of town. Everyone would go there to bake their bread.

What do you get when you cross a kitchen **cabinet** and a commander of the Starship Enterprise?

★ *Jean-Luc **Placard*** (Picard; un placard = cabinet)

What do the French use to keep their **dishes** soft and smooth?

★ ***Vaisselle**-line Intensive Care* (Vaseline; la vaisselle = dishes, dinnerware)

What did the French lady ask the furniture salesman when she was ready to buy a **couch**?

★ *"**Canapé** with a credit card?"* (can I pay; un canapé = couch)

What happened to the French thief who stole a
casserole dish?

★ *He got* **cocotte.** *(caught; une cocotte = casserole dish, Dutch
oven)*

FUN FACT: "Ma cocotte" is a term of endearment for honey,
dear, or sweetie.

How did the French woman react when she saw her new
dishwasher?

★ *It was* **lave-vaisselle** *at first sight. (love; un lave-vaisselle =
dishwasher; la vaisselle = dishes, dinnerware)*

What do you get when you cross the Wright Brothers
with a French kitchen **sink**?

★ *the history of* **évier**-*tion (aviaton; un évier = sink)*

FUN FACT: France is a leader in aviation. The Mirage, Carvelle,
Concorde, Airiane, and the Airbus are some of its planes. The
Airbus 380 will seat 555 passengers.

What do the French call a picture of an **armchair**?

★ *a* **fauteuil**-*graphe (photograph; un fauteuil = upholstered
armchair)*

What are French people doing when they sweep their
floors?

★ **balai** *dancing (belly; un balai = broom)*

What French king was always sitting down?

★ *Louis* **Chaise** *(Seize = sixteen, the sixteenth; une chaise = chair)*

FUN FACT: Louis XIV had strict rules about chairs. Only the king and queen could sit in chairs with arms. Their children sat in chairs without arms. The nobles got the stools.

Where do French people eat pasta and sleep?

★ *in a ravio-**lit*** *(ravioli; un lit = bed)*

FUN FACT: Historically, French beds were short, even for tall kings and nobles. People slept almost sitting up, propped up by pillows because they were afraid the "death spirits" would invade their bodies if they lay flat on their backs.

What do the French say when there is only one clean **sheet** left?

★ *"This is the last **drap**."* *(straw; un drap = sheet)*

FUN FACT: The word "drapery" is related to the word "drap," originally a fabric that was hung. The French word for flag, "drapeau," is also from the same root.

What is the opening movement of a French symphony about a bed warmer called?

★ *a **couverture*** *(overture; une couverture = blanket)*

FUN FACT: Toussaint-Louverture (1743–1803) was a slave who with no military experience led a revolution that ousted Napoléon from Saint-Domingue, now Haiti. He also led Haiti to its independence.

Where in the bedroom do French people put their **noodles** before going to sleep?

★ *on a table de **nouilles*** *(une table de nuit = nightstand; des nouilles = noodles)*

From which American city do the French import their **rug**s?

★ ***Tapis**-ka, Kansas* *(Topeka; un tapis = rug)*

FUN FACT: A "tapis" put on a wall is a "tapisserie" or tapestry. Gobelins has been the premier French tapestry manufacturer since the fifteenth century.

What early-'60s TV show told tales about strange things that happened in French bathrooms?

★ *"The **Toilettes** Zone"* *("The Twilight Zone"; les toilettes = toilet [always plural])*

FUN FACT: Paris has 420 modern high-tech toilet cabins on its sidewalks called "sanisettes." The fee is 0.40 euros (about 50 cents), but in 2007 they will be free. After you leave and the door shuts, water flushes out and sanitizes the whole inside of the facility. You don't want to get caught inside!

What do French children shout as they race each other to **bed**?

★ *"Au **lit** au lit in free."* *("Olly olly in free"; au lit = to bed)*

FUN FACT: Louis XIV had 413 beds.

Which American ambassador to Paris was careful not to fly a kite while soaking in the **tub**?

★ **Baignoire** Franklin *(Ben; une baignoire = bathtub)*

FUN FACT: Benjamin Franklin spent 1777 to 1785 in France as an ambassador. He inspired copycat lightning rods all over Paris. He brought the first bathtub back to the United States and found ways to improve it.

Why didn't the French home owner have to buy **lightbulb**s?

★ *Because there was an **ampoule** supply in the closet.*
(ample; une ampoule = lightbulb)

What does a French person say when an **iron** is stolen?

★ *"No **fer**!"* *("No fair!"; un fer = iron [the metal]; iron [for ironing])*

FUN FACT: *L'Homme au masque de fer* (*The Man in the Iron Mask*) is the Alexandre Dumas novel about a mysterious prisoner in the Tower of London forced to wear an iron mask. It is believed he was the twin of the French king, Louis XVI.

Where in a French house are people always smiling?

★ *in the **grinier*** *(grin; un grenier= attic)*

FUN FACT: The "grenier" is a loft where farmers stored grains. It gradually became the word for the upper level of a house where unused possessions are stored.

MUSIC

★

La musique

What do you get when you cross Colgate with a large French wind instrument?

★ a **tuba** toothpaste *(un tuba = tuba)*

Why was the French drummer late for his band's rehearsal?

★ He had to recharge his **batterie**. *(battery; la batterie = drum set)*

What French children's song is about cooking a hammerhead?

★ **"Frire Shark"** *("Frère Jacques"; frire = to fry)*

What is the most musical part of the French language?

★ the **gramm-air** *(la grammaire = grammar; un air = melody)*

What do you get when you cross Thomas Edison with Claude Debussy?

★ *"Prelude to the Afternoon of a Phone"* *(Faun; "Prélude à l'après-midi d'un faune" = "Prelude to the Afternoon of a Faun" by Debussy)*

FUN FACT: Claude Debussy (1862–1918) created pretty, flowing melodies. He also wrote "La mer" (The Sea) and "Clair de lune" ("Light of the Moon"). Debussy failed his virtuoso piano exam twice, so he composed instead.

What French singer owns a wireless telephone store?

★ *MC Cellular (MC Solaar)*

FUN FACT: MC Solaar (1969–) from Dakar, Senegal, is France's top rapper. He was born Claude M'Barali. His mellow, soulful rap, catchy grooves, antiviolent themes, and clever poetry have won him world fame. His hits include "Caroline," "Victime de la mode," and "Nouveau western."

Who traveled around medieval France singing songs about **holes**?

★ the **trous**-badours *(troubadours; un trou = hole)*

FUN FACT: Troubadours in southern France wandered from town to town in the twelfth and thirteenth centuries, reporting the latest news or gossip in songs.

What happened to the French song lyricist who was a model inmate in prison?

★ He was let out on **parole**. *(parole; la parole = lyrics of a song)*

What legendary French singer sang romantic songs about a rice dish?

★ *Édith Pilaf* (Piaf; rice pilaf)

> **FUN FACT:** Édith Piaf (1915–1963) is France's legendary singer who performed in the 1940s and 1950s and had international fame. When she was nine, she sang "La Marseillaise," the French national anthem, on the streets of Paris for money. She was blind from age three to age seven due to meningitis, but regained her sight.

When did the composer of French dance-hall music say he would return to his office?

★ *in ten minutes, but he was* **Offenbach** *sooner* (often back)

> **FUN FACT:** Jacques Offenbach (1819–1880) composed the famous music for the French cancan, invented in 1830. His ninety-seven humorous operettas with dialogue mixed in began musical theater on Broadway. It's rumored that Offenbach once fired a valet because he showed no sense of rhythm when he beat the composer's clothes to freshen them up.

What did people in medieval France listen to after a big dinner?

★ *a* **chanson** *digest* (une chanson de geste = song about a heroic deed)

> **FUN FACT:** A "chanson de geste" is a song about battles, heroes, courtly love, or chivalry that was sung by the roaming troubadours during the Middle Ages.

What social French event does Bullwinkle attend when he's in France?

★ a **bal** moose-ette *(moose; bal musette = dance with French accordion music)*

FUN FACT: A "musette" is a type of accordion. Lively musette music symbolizes France, and is played on commercials and TV shows when scenes of France appear.

Dancing at the bal moose-ette

What did Jean-Baptiste Lully say when he was asked to hum his new melody and he forgot it?

★ *"Give me a minute. I'll think **gavotte**."* *(of it; une gavotte = classical dance music)*

FUN FACT: The "gavotte" was a seventeenth-century dance done in a circle with skipping steps. It was popular at the court of Louis XIV. The court composer, Jean-Baptiste Lully, used the gavotte in the ballets performed in the evenings for the king.

What did the French-Polish composer of pieces for piano students have to do before he wrote down his music?

★ **Chopin** *his pencil* (sharpen; Frédéric Chopin = French-Polish piano virtuoso)

> **FUN FACT:** Frédéric Chopin (1810–1849) wrote waltzes, nocturnes, sonatas, scherzos, preludes, mazurkas, and impromptus. He was a piano teacher and composed "études" for practicing piano techniques. Chopin shaved one side of his face but had a beard on the other side. He thought that was practical because audiences only saw one side when he played concerts.

What did the French maestro say when the orchestra rushed the classical piece?

★ *"That's **sonate** how you're supposed to play it."* (That's not; une sonate = sonata)

How do you close the cover of a French **CD case**?

★ *You **pochette**.* (push it; une pochette = CD case)

What was the favorite Italian dish of the composer of "Boléro?"

★ **Ravel**-*ioli* (ravioli; Ravel = Impressionist composer)

> **FUN FACT:** Maurice Ravel (1875–1937) was a piano virtuoso and composer. "Boléro" was on the sound track of the 1979 movie *10* with Dudley Moore and Bo Derek. Ravel had long sideburns, was always well-groomed, wore fancy ties, and liked mechanical birds and gadgets.

How would you describe the composer of *Carmen* when he was working?

★ **Bizet** as a bee *(busy; Bizet = composer of symphonies and operas)*

FUN FACT: Georges Bizet (1838–1875) entered the Conservatory of Music at age nine and wrote his first symphony at age seventeen. His opera *Carmen* is a tragic story about a Spanish gypsy. Two of its songs, "March of the Toreadors" and "Habanera," are very familiar melodies to most people.

Why can French people put their **CDs** anywhere, even in small places?

★ Because they are so **compact**. *(compact; un compact = CD)*

FUN FACT: A French CD is called "un compact" or "un CD." A hit song is "une tube." Two French radio stations that play the top hits are NRJ (sounds like "énergie") and Skyrock.

In which musical instrument do the French put ice cream?

★ in a **cornet** *(un cornet = ice-cream cone; un cor net = a clean horn; un cor = horn)*

FUN FACT: A French "glacier" or ice-cream maker will ask if you want "une," "deux," or "trois boules" (1, 2, or 3 scoops). The most popular ice cream in Paris is made by Berthillon, on the Île Saint-Louis.

What do you call a French handyman's list of all the things he can fix?

★ *his repair-toire* (un répertoire = list of learned songs or activities that can be performed)

FUN FACT: The word "bricolage" means do-it-yourself projects or odd jobs around the house for a handyman to do. French department stores have big "bricolage" departments.

Where does a French **bass** player wait for his ride?

★ *at a **basse** stop* (bus; une basse = bass guitar)

FUN FACT: Louis XIV played the guitar.

How do French vocal coaches say good-bye to their students?

★ *"Au re-**voix**."* (au revoir = good-bye; une voix = voice)

NUMBERS

Les nombres

What French number can keep a secret?

★ *Ten, because it's **dix**-creet.* (discreet; dix = ten)

What French number is materialistic?

★ *Eleven, because it **onze** a lot of stuff.* (owns; onze = eleven)

What is the major character flaw of the French number **twenty**?

★ *its **vingt**-nity* (vanity; vingt = twenty)

What French number is inflexible?

★ *Seven, because it's **sept** in its ways.* (set; sept = seven)

What French boy band's fame went below sea level?

★ 'N **Cinq** *(sank; 'N Sync; cinq = five)*

FUN FACT: "France 5" (formerly "La Cinquième) is a French TV station created in 2002. TV5 is a worldwide satellite station in French.

What beef dish is prepared for **nine** French people at a time?

★ beef stroga-**neuf** *(stroganoff; neuf = nine)*

What did the French number **three** say when it was skipped in the countdown?

★ *"That was very **trois**-matic."* *(traumatic; trois = three)*

FUN FACT: "Les trois coups" (the three knocks) are made with a baton in French theaters as the curtain rises to signal the audience that the play is about to begin. This has been a tradition for centuries.

Why didn't the French boy turn in his math homework?

★ *He couldn't do **huit**. (do it; huit = eight)*

What does a French newspaper call it when a person turns **forty**?

★ a **quarante** event *(current; quarante = forty)*

FUN FACT: *Le Monde* (1944) and *Le Figaro* (1826) are France's two major newspapers.

Which French king ran a tourist agency for felines?

⋆ *Louis Cat Tours* (quatorze = fourteen). *The tour included the Paris Catacombs.*

FUN FACT: Louis XIV became king at age four but didn't take the throne until he was thirteen. Louis XIII was the father of Louis XIV who was the great-grandfather of Louis XV who was the grandfather of Louis XVI who had two children named Louis.

What four-time Heavyweight Champion was obsessed with the French number **twenty-two**?

⋆ E. **Vingt-Deux** Holyfield *(Evander; vingt-deux = twenty-two)*

What French number helps to lower cholesterol?

⋆ *Seven, because it's polyun-***sept***-urated.* (polyunsaturated; sept = seven)

FUN FACT: A French proverb says, "Il faut penser sept fois avant de se mettre en colère ("You should think seven times before getting mad").

What do you call a French performer who can do **twenty** voices for his dummy?

⋆ *a* **vingt**-*triloquist* (ventriloquist; vingt = twenty)

In which Ontario city do **thirty**-year-old French people live?

⋆ *in* **Trente**-*o* (Toronto; trente = thirty)

What game played at Versailles required children to get the king's permission before making a move, or else they were out?

★ *Louis Says* *(Louis XVI; seize = sixteen, the sixteenth)*

FUN FACT: In 1988 Louis XVI, who was guillotined in 1793, got another trial. It was a trial reenactment on TV. The viewers acquitted him with 55 percent of the vote.

What do the French call it when someone counts from twelve to fourteen?

★ **treize**-*passing* *(trespassing; treize = thirteen)*

FUN FACT: The number treize (thirteen) is a number "malchanceux" (unlucky) in France. "La triskaidékaphobie" is the fear of the number thirteen.

What French number has the most fiber?

★ *Eight, because it's 100 percent whole* **huit***.* *(wheat; huit = eight)*

Which French sandwich condiment comes in **fifteen** varieties?

★ **Quinze** *Mayonnaise (Caines; quinze = fifteen)*

RESTAURANT

Le restaurant . . . Miam! Miam!

In what kind of French restaurant do people hug a lot?

★ in an em**brasserie** *(brasserie = type of casual French restaurant; embrasser = to embrace, kiss)*

FUN FACT: A brasserie serves drinks and light food or meals. It usually has rich mahogany booths, white tablecloths, large mirrors on the walls, and chandeliers. It comes from the word "brasser," which means "to brew." The brasseries came to France from Germany.

When French geography teachers go to a restaurant, how do they order?

★ à la **carte** *(une carte = menu, map)*

FUN FACT: The "carte" is the correct term for the list of foods served at a French restaurant.

What did the French restaurant owner exclaim as he watched the lion speed across the lake in a boat with oars?

★ *"Look at that beast row!"* (bistro; un bistro = French café)

FUN FACT: Speaking of speed, it's said that the word "bistro" was born when Russian soldiers ran into French cafés asking for fast service. The Russian word for "fast," which sounds like "bw-EE-stroh," turned into "bistro."

What do you call the people who spend hours sitting in front of French cafés?

★ **terrasse**-*trials* (terrestrials; une terrasse = sidewalk café)

FUN FACT: A customer may sit at a table on the "terrasse" with a cup of coffee or a cocoa for as long as he or she wants to, reading, relaxing, or watching people.

What do French **waiter**s who have been dating do when they break up?

★ **serveur** *all ties* (sever; un serveur = waiter, server)

FUN FACT: The term "Garçon" (Boy), once used to get a server's attention, is no longer used. Customers now say, "Monsieur" (or "Madame") to get a server's attention. Paris servers race in the streets in April with glasses and bottles on their trays.

If you are a French **fork**, can you make another fork fall in love with you?

★ *No, you just can't* **fourchette.** *(force it; une fourchette = fork)*

What does a French server give to all customers at every table?

★ a **commande** performance *(command; une commande = order)*

> **FUN FACT:** In seventeenth-century France, it was customary for aristocrats to bring their own servers when invited to dinner.

What kind of work do servers in French restaurants do?

★ **menu**-al labor *(manual labor; menu = meal deal)*

> **FUN FACT:** A "menu" in French restaurants is a meal deal (menu à prix fixe) for a set price. It includes a choice of an appetizer, a main dish, and a dessert.

What do the French call gourmet **cooking** for horses?

★ oat **cuisine** *(haute cuisine = gourmet cooking)*

> **FUN FACT:** Haute cuisine ("high" or gourmet cooking), is said to have begun with Napoléon. It involves many courses, sauces, butter and cream, quality ingredients, and artistic presentation.

What employee of a French restaurant always measures up?

★ the **mètre** d' *(maître d' = headwaiter; un mètre = metric measure equal to 39 inches)*

> **FUN FACT:** A maître d' is the "master of the hall" who greets people at a restaurant and assigns tables to servers.

What does a French woman say she does before she sits down for a meal?

★ ***Assiette*** *the table."* (I set; une assiette = plate)

FUN FACT: Nicolas Fouquet wanted to impress Louis XIV so he served a meal in his honor on gold dinnerware. The king was highly insulted by the show-off noble, and he sent him to prison.

Why did the French waiter who was stealing a **tablecloth** get caught?

★ *He was taking a **nappe**.* (une nappe = tablecloth)

From where in Italy do French restaurants get their coffee **cup**s?

★ ***Tasse**-cany* (Tuscany [Italy]; une tasse = cup)

What Italian designer makes French **glass**ware?

★ ***Verre**-sace* (Versace; un verre = [drinking] glass)

Where do French fish eat with **spoon**s?

★ *in an a-**cuillère**-ium* (aquarium; une cuillère = spoon)

What is a French **cook**'s favorite cruise ship activity?

★ ***Chef**-fleboard* (shuffleboard; un chef = chef)

FUN FACT: The French chef, Karl Fritz Vatel, planned an extravagant three-day gala with three thousand guests to honor Louis XIV. The fresh fish that he had ordered, however, didn't arrive. Vatel was so upset he ended his life during the event.

What do French people say when they give their dogs a treat to chew on?

★ *"Bone appétit!"* *(bon appétit = enjoy your meal)*

FUN FACT: Julia Child attended the École Cordon Bleu cooking school in Paris and became a Master Chef. She ended her TV show with "Bon appétit."

What would a French chef say to quiet everyone down during the first phase of a trial?

★ *"**Hors d'œuvre** in the court."* *(Order; un hors d'œuvre = appetizer)*

FUN FACT: The term "hors d'œuvre" came from French architects. If they added a separate small building that wasn't in the original plans, they called it "hors d'œuvre" (outside the work). Chefs started using the term for snacks eaten "outside" the main dish.

The French chef silences a noisy—and hungry—courtroom.

What do you call the minestrone that was served to the French courtroom's deliberating body?

★ *a soupe du juror* (la soupe du jour = the soup of the day)

FUN FACT: "Soup" and "supper" are from the French "sop" (bread used to soak up the liquids) and "souper" (to have supper). Starving peasants of the seventeenth century were able to eat from one pig for almost a year. They boiled the bones and added bread crusts (croûtons) to help fill them up.

What do you call a French entrepreneur who makes a fortune in broth?

★ *a **bouillon**-aire* (billionaire; le bouillon = clear broth)

In what French sport do soup makers from Southern France hit a ball with a fish?

★ ***bouillabaisse**-ball* (baseball; la bouillabaisse = Mediterranean seafood stew)

What do you call a French toddler who has learned to appreciate a **liver appetizer**?

★ ***pâté** trained* (potty; le pâté = ground-liver paste)

FUN FACT: Pâté, meaning "paste," is a liver spread molded in a loaf pan and sliced or spread on small toasts or crackers. "Pâté de foie gras" made with goose liver is an expensive delicacy. Geese are purposely overfed to increase the size of their livers.

Which French wrestler was known for eating a **small appetizer** just before his match?

⋆ **Entrée** the Giant *(André the Giant = French wrestler; une entrée = small appetizer like soup, veggies, fish, melon, or quiche)*

   FUN FACT: An entrée in the United States is the main dish. The "plat principal" is the main dish in France. André the Giant (1946–1993) at age twelve was 6'3" and weighed 200 pounds due to natural growth hormones. He reached 7'4" and 500 pounds. He wrestled Hulk Hogan and played the Bionic Bigfoot in "The Six Million Dollar Man."

How did the Frenchman ask his wife for another slice of the egg and ham pie?

⋆ *"Give me a little **quiche**, will you, hon?"* *(kiss; une quiche = egg pie)*

   FUN FACT: A quiche has eggs, cheese, cream, and other ingredients like vegetables, seafood, or ham. It's baked in a pie shell. Quiche lorraine has bacon and onions.

What do you get when you cross Nestlé and a chicken?

⋆ *cocoa vin (le coq au vin = chicken stew cooked in a wine sauce)*

What is a cross between a conceited French ape named James and a scallop dish?

⋆ *cocky singe Jacques (les coquilles Saint-Jacques = scallops; un singe = monkey)*

What did the French beanstalk giant shout when he smelled a steak?

★ *"Fe Fi **Faux-filet** Fum!"* *("Fe, Fi, Fo, Fum!"; un faux-filet = sirloin steak)*

What is the competition between MacDonald's and Quick in France called?

★ *a bur-**guerre*** *(burger, une guerre = war; Quick = hamburger chain in France)*

FUN FACT: Quick sells the Giant, Suprême Cheese, Quick 'n Toast, chicken dips, and salads with Camembert cheese, olives, and goat cheese. The sixty-six McDonald's restaurants in Paris sell "le Big Mac" and "le Royal." The slogan "I'm lovin' it" is "C'est tout ce que j'aime" in France.

What do French frogs eat with their burgers?

★ *French flies* *(French fries)*

FUN FACT: In France "pommes frites" are fried chunks of potato. Thomas Jefferson, who visited France often, really liked the French-style potatoes and brought them to the United States. The "frites," or shoestring fries, came later.

What dish does a French president prefer not to order at the end of his term?

★ *lame duck à l'orange* *(duck à l'orange = duck with orange sauce)*

What is the favorite sandwich of French frogs?

★ *a croak-monsieur* (un croque-monsieur = melted cheese–
covered sandwich)

FUN FACT: A croque-monsieur is a ham sandwich covered with
cheese and grilled in a broiler. A croque-madame is a croque-
monsieur with a fried egg on top of it. A croque-odile—you sure
don't want to see that in a French restaurant.

Which French steak is always sleepy?

★ *a filet min-yawn* (un filet mignon = a cut, boneless, tender piece
of beef)

What kind of chicken in France is in the shape of little jackets?

★ *chicken coat-lettes* (une côtelette = cutlet)

What did the crowd shout when the French snail took the lead at Daytona?

★ *"Look at that brown NASCAR go!"* (escargot; un escargot =
snail)

Why don't French people have to pay when they order **fried chicken**?

★ *Because it's **poulet frit**.* (pronounced "free"; le poulet frit =
fried chicken)

What do you get when you cross a French salad with the "Wheel of Fortune"?

★ *Vanna Grette* *(Vanna White; la vinaigrette = dressing with vinegar, olive oil, and mustard)*

FUN FACT: "Wheel of Fortune" is "Roue de la Fortune" in France. Vinaigrette (vin = wine; aigre = sour) is the most common French dressing. People make it fresh in their homes and put it on lettuce.

What kind of cheese does Mick Jagger order in a French restaurant?

★ *le Roquefort* *(le rock fort = loud rock music)*

FUN FACT: Roquefort cheese is a very strong bleu cheese made with ewe's milk and a blue mold found in caves. It comes from the town of Roquefort-sur-Soulzon.

According to a French pastry chef, what is the weather report?

★ *"It's going to be éclair day."* *(clear; un éclair = cream-filled pastry)*

FUN FACT: An "éclair" is an oblong puff pastry shell filled with a vanilla cream or whipped cream and topped with chocolate or coffee frosting. It means "lightening bolt."

What is a list of flavors on a French ice-cream parlor menu called?

★ *a glace-ary* *(glossary; la glace = ice cream)*

What must a French pastry chef do when he hasn't made breakfast rolls in a long time?

★ **brioche** *up on his skills (brush up; une brioche = a breakfast roll)*

FUN FACT: A brioche is a sweet roll made with flour, yeast, eggs, and butter.

What did the French pastry chef say when he held the tray with two cream puffs in front of the customer?

★ *"You have two **chous**." (to choose; un chou = cream puff)*

FUN FACT: Chou paste is used to make many French pastries like cream puffs and éclairs. Profiteroles is a dessert with three small cream puffs topped with chocolate sauce. You could say that French pastry chefs are in "chou" business. "Chou" also means "cabbage."

Madame Goizet can't decide which dessert to order.

Which Elton John song is about a French donut that played on a New York football team?

★ **"Beignet** *and the Jets"* (un beignet = donut)

FUN FACT: Beignets are like donuts, except that they are rectangular and have no holes. They are deep-fried and covered with powdered sugar. Beignets are a specialty at the Café du Monde in New Orleans.

What accumulates on the teeth of French people when they eat fruit pastries?

★ **tarte**-*ar* (tartar; une tarte = small fruit-filled pastry)

FUN FACT: A French "tarte" has a crust shell filled with vanilla cream and has fresh fruits on top of it. Strawberry and multifruit tarts are the most popular tarts.

Which Greek playwright wrote tragedies about a French dessert that sometimes flops?

★ **Soufflé**-*cles* (Sophocles; un soufflé = baked dish that inflates)

What is the famous quote of the self-centered pastry chef of Louis XIV?

★ *"La* **tarte***, c'est moi!"* (L'État = the state; une tarte = a small fruit-filled pastry)

FUN FACT: Louis XIV, the "sun king" of France, said, "L'État, c'est moi" ("I am the state"). He believed he had absolute and divine power to rule France and was king for an incredible seventy-two years.

What French dessert gets rid of bad breath?

⋆ *poires Belle-haleine (poires Belle-Hélène = pear and ice cream dessert; belle = beautiful; la haleine = breath)*

FUN FACT: This dessert was invented for an operetta by Offenbach called *La Belle Hélène* about Helen of Troy. It's made with vanilla ice cream, pear halves, and chocolate sauce. Crêpes can be filled with the same ingredients, too. "C'est délicieux!"

What crime is committed when a French chef copies another chef's small finger cakes?

⋆ **Petit four***-gery (petty forgery; un petit four = tiny bite-size cake, small oven)*

FUN FACT: Petits fours are small finger cakes. They are square or in other shapes, too. After icing is put on them, they are decorated.

What is looking at a delicious French **cake** in a pastry shop window and not being able to eat it?

⋆ **Torte***-ture (torture; une torte = a fancy cake)*

FUN FACT: A torte is a rich cake that can have one layer or more. It may have cream layers and fresh fruits like blueberries, strawberries, raspberries, or kiwi on top of it. Some have rich fudge icing on them.

What do the French call dishes used for serving **ice cream**?

⋆ **glace***-ware (glassware; la glace = ice cream)*

What play is about two French chefs who patiently hang out while their **cake** bakes?

★ Waiting for **Gâteau** *(Godot, a Samuel Beckett play; un gâteau = cake)*

FUN FACT: In *Waiting for Godot*, Vladimir and Estragon wait for Godot on a deserted road for the entire play. He never comes, but they are afraid to leave. A "petit gâteau" is a "cookie." Cookie Monster shouts "Gâââââââteau" in France.

How does the diabolic French pastry chef plan to destroy Superman?

★ *By exposing him to **crêpes** tonight. (kryptonite; les crêpes = thin pancakes)*

FUN FACT: Crêpes are topped with sugar, jam, Nutella, ice cream, or fruit compotes. They can be filled with eggs, cheese, seafood, meats, sauces, and dessert ingredients.

Why do so many people in Montana eat French **waffle**s?

★ *Because they live in the **gaufre** state. (gopher; une gaufre = waffle)*

FUN FACT: A "gaufre" is a waffle topped with sugar, Nutella, jam, maple syrup, or ice cream. It's a common French street food.

Why doesn't a French cockroach drink Pepsi?

★ *Because it's a **coca**-roach. (cockroach; un coca = Coca-Cola)*

What are two favorite desserts of French cats?

★ *a purr-fait and a chat-lotte* (un parfait = parfait; une charlotte = charlotte)

FUN FACT: A parfait has layers of ice cream or pudding, syrups, and whipped cream. A charlotte is a mold of vertical sponge fingers with pudding and fruit inside.

What Brazilian dance are French people doing when they drink a **beverage**?

★ the **boisson** nova (bossa nova; une boisson = drink)

What do French people call it when they raise a slice of egg-covered bread in the air?

★ *a French Toast*

FUN FACT: The French say "Chin chin" as a toast when they tap glasses together. French toast is "pain perdu" (lost bread). Cooks in the past didn't want to waste the stale bread so they moistened it with milk and eggs and fried it.

Which two beverages do French martial arts instructors drink?

★ *judo pomme and kara-thé* (le jus de pomme = apple juice; le karaté = karate; le thé = tea)

FUN FACT: There is a juice in France with a spicy jolt called Cactus. It comes in Original, Hot, and Energy.

What credential is required for vendors in France to sell mineral **water**?

★ *a l'**eau** degree* (law; l'eau = water; l'eau minérale = mineral water)

FUN FACT: French people drink bottled water, either carbonated ("gazeuse") or uncarbonated ("non-gazeuse"). Popular brands are Vittel, Volvic, Évian, Badoit, Contrex, and Perrier.

What kind of Spanish coffee is served in French restaurants?

★ ***café** olé* (café au lait = coffee drink)

FUN FACT: Café au lait is half coffee and half milk.

What is the body of novels, poems, and short stories that French cows read called?

★ ***lait**-térature* (literature; le lait = milk)

FUN FACT: Milk in France comes in rectangular "briques" that look like soy milk containers or large juice boxes. They come in six-packs and need no refrigeration until opened.

What is the standard cheer of people who drink French mineral water?

★ *"Hip hip **Perrier**!"* ("Hip hip hurray!")

FUN FACT: Today Perrier is a company of Nestlé. It's the #1 carbonated water in the world and is sold in 120 countries.

What do the French call it when a cow jumps up and stuffs a basketball through a hoop?

★ *a **lait**-up (layup; le lait = milk)*

Going for a Lait-up

What do the French call **water** that is disguised with syrups?

★ *incognit-**eau** (incognito; l'eau = water)*

> **FUN FACT:** Teisseire makes flavored syrups that can be added to water, sodas, lemonade, or any other beverage to create designer drinks. Some of their flavors are: peach, mint, raspberry, strawberry, apple, licorice, lemon, blackberry, grenadine, and cherry.

How often do French people drink a beverage made with water and green mint syrup?

★ *once a **menthe** (month; une menthe = mint and water drink)*

Which actress who played the U.S. president on TV drinks a French citrus-flavored soda?

★ **Orangina** Davis *(Geena; Orangina = orange soda)*

   FUN FACT: Orangina is an orange juice–based soda sold in France. It comes in a short, round glass bottle, in plastic bottles, and in cans. Orangina arrived in the United States in 1985.

What three kinds of French **tea** are very patriotic?

★ *liber-**thé**, égali-**thé**, fraterni-**thé*** *(Liberté, égalité, fraternité = Liberty, equality, fraternity)*

   FUN FACT: "Liberté, égalité, fraternité" is the motto of France.

What is a French **donkey**'s favorite juice?

★ *jus d'**âne**-anas (un ananas = pineapple juice; un âne = donkey)*

LA FIN!